ADVINDICATION

AFFIRMING THE PILLARS OF OUR FAITH

ADVINDICATION

AFFIRMING THE PILLARS OF OUR FAITH

BY

DOUG BATCHELOR

Roseville, CA

Published by
Amazing Facts, Inc.
PO Box 1058
Roseville, CA 95678-8058

Edited by Dr. Herbert Douglass, Anthony Lester
Copyedited by Steven Winn, Leslie Kay
Cover Design by Haley Trimmer
Layout by Greg Solie - Altamont Graphics

Library of Congress Cataloging-in-Publication Data

Batchelor, Doug, 1957-
  Advindication : affirming the pillars of our faith / by Doug Batchelor.
    p. cm.
  Includes bibliographical references and index.
  ISBN 1-58019-159-2 (alk. paper)
  1. Seventh-Day Adventists--Apologetic works. I. Title.

BX6154.B375 2004
286.7'32--dc22
                        2004016612

---

04 05 06 07 08 • 5 4 3 2 1

TABLE OF CONTENTS

INTRODUCTION

Have you ever wondered what exactly is a Seventh-day Adventist? I once saw a video of interviews conducted on the streets of New York City that primarily asked, "What do you think a Seventh-day Adventist is?"

I listened to many creative answers, such as, "Aren't you the religion that doesn't believe in blood transfusions?" As a pastor, I was embarrassed to realize that only a handful of people had even a scant understanding of Seventh-day Adventists. (My hopes perked a bit when I finally heard one person say, "I know! You're the ones that go to church on Saturday!")

After realizing that many people have no idea what Seventh-day Adventists are all about, I wanted to write a book that would 1) briefly introduce some answers to this intriguing question, and 2) address many of the misconceptions. I want this book to help illuminate those answers in a way that makes sense to me—and, I trust, for you.

When I gave my heart to the Lord and accepted Jesus into my life, I realized that there were many Christian denominations in the world that claim to believe in the Bible. I remember praying, "Lord, I want to know the truth based on Your Word."

I am now a Seventh-day Adventist, but it is vitally important to note that my loyalty is first given to God and not to the organization. It does provide a wonderful place for me to share my convictions about the Bible, but to be very honest, I sometimes do not want to be a Seventh-day Adventist. I do not always like being different—I am already different enough. However, I am compelled by logic and by a burning need to be honest with my soul. I became convinced that I should become a Seventh-day Adventist because this was the only denomination that could provide clear and satisfying answers to my legitimate questions.

Of course, I am not the only person who has had to face the challenge posed by the large number of denominations in the Christian church. Many scholarly books have been written, which attempt to dissect religious groups and classify the differences that make each group unique. These studies often narrow religions down into categories such as Protestant, Catholic, or cult.

Dr. Walter Martin, author of the book *The Kingdom of the Cults,* identifies and deals with the teachings of various religious cults. He offers practical information dealing with a variety of religious persuasions. While it is obvious that he is not quite sure what to do with Seventh-day Adventism, he does classify it as a Christian-based denomination, stating that "it has been included in this volume because for over a century, Adventism has carried the stigma of being called a non-Christian cult. Nobody can really pinpoint the stigma except to say, 'Well, they are just so different.' "

Dr. Martin continues, "Hence it is our position that Seventh-day Adventism as a denomination is essentially Christian in the sense that all denominations and groups professing Christianity are Christian if they conform to the councils of the Christian church. But this does not mean that all Baptists, all Methodists, all Episcopalians, all Lutherans or all Seventh-day Adventists are Christians."

What he is saying here is that there are some Seventh-day Adventists who are cultish, but this holds true in any denomination.

I will not deny that Seventh-day Adventists are different, but we are not a cult. So I want to focus on the most common accusations against Adventism, that classify us as a cult. I hope that this effort will produce constructive dialogue and help both current Adventists and anyone interested in my church to better understand what we are all about.

Chapter One

ADVENTISTS AND THE LAW

The very first step in grasping the fundamentals of what seems to make a Seventh-day Adventist different, is understanding our relationship to the law of God.

One of the best ways to develop this understanding is to ask what seems at first to be a very small question. Yet it is a question that has a huge impact on every religious persuasion that claims to be Bible-based.

The question: Is obedience legalism? When we distinguish between the different denominations, we usually do so by picking out a teaching or two that is unique to a certain group—whether our understanding of the sect, or its teaching, is completely accurate or not.

For instance, what comes to mind when you think of Charismatics or Pentecostals? Typically, we think of "speaking in tongues." When we think of Baptists, we almost automatically think of "baptism by immersion," and when we think of Presbyterians, "predestination" comes to mind. Wouldn't you agree?

Adventism is no different. When people think of what distinguishes Adventists from other mainstream denominations, they quickly identify our position of keeping the seventh-day Sabbath, which in turn leads to suspicions of legalism.

For many, Seventh-day Adventists have an unusual approach to understanding the law and grace. When Adventists talk about obeying the seventh-day Sabbath, people often ask, "Why?" We answer, "It's one of the Ten Commandments." They say, "You're legalistic! We are not under the law; we are under grace."

A LEGAL-WHAT?

What is a legalist anyway? It's an emotionally charged word that is often thrown around too casually. Fortunately, Jesus highlighted the term while delivering His Sermon on the Mount. He said to the Pharisees: "And when you pray, you shall not be like the hypocrites. For they love to pray standing in the synagogues and on the corners of the streets, that they may be seen by men. Assuredly, I say to you, they have their reward" (Matthew 6:5).

It's vitally important to understand that Jesus is not condemning prayer, but rather the attitude in which the pharisaical prayer is offered. A few verses earlier, Jesus said: "Therefore, when you do a charitable deed, do not sound a trumpet before you as the hypocrites do in the synagogues and in the streets, that they may have glory from men. Assuredly, I say to you, they have their reward" (Matthew 6:2). Later, He emphasized: "Moreover, when you fast, do not be like the hypocrites, with a sad countenance. For they disfigure their faces that they may appear to men to be fasting. Assuredly, I say to you, they have their reward" (Matthew 6:16).

Through these messages, Christ is teaching us that what is in our hearts is what counts. He identifies the difference between true religion and its counterfeit—or, to put it another way, between love and legalism. Legalism looks at the exterior; legalists primarily concern themselves with outward compliance, both in themselves and in others. In contrast, Christ says that it is an inward change of heart that He desires.

The motive is the issue when discussing legalism. A legalist can be defined as a person who may be outwardly embracing the right issues, while simultaneously measuring himself or judging another person by external behavior instead of focusing on the motive, or root, of the problem.

BEFORE SINAI, THE LAW

Now that we have clarified the definition of legalism, we can better understand the real purpose of God's Law.

Here is a very important question: How long do you think the Law of God has existed?

Some argue that God's Law began with the delivery of the Ten Commandments on the top of Mount Sinai, but I respectfully disagree. I believe that the principles upon which the Ten Commandments are based are eternal, and thus have always been in existence.

No doubt the angels never thought about specific laws of God before Satan introduced sin into the universe. Obviously, lying, stealing and murder weren't even considered in an environment in which every action was governed by love.

But on earth, hundreds of years before the Ten Commandments were written in stone, God spoke of them while referring to Abraham: "Abraham obeyed My voice, and kept My charge, My commandments, my statutes, and My laws" (Genesis 26:5). But even earlier, in Genesis 4:7, God said to Cain, "If you do well, will you not be accepted? And if you do not do well, sin lies at the door."

In the very beginning, long before Jews existed, God refers to sin. Yet it is not possible to have sin when there is no law!

Paul adds further light on these principles concerning sin and the Law. In Romans 4:15, he wrote, "Because the law brings about wrath; where there is no law, there is no transgression." And if that isn't clear enough, he puts it another way in Romans 5:13: "For until the law sin was in the world, but sin is not imputed when there is no law." According to Paul, God has always had a Law.

The story of Joseph illustrates this point well. When Joseph was tempted by Potiphar's wife to commit adultery, Joseph knew it went against the Law of God, long before Mount Sinai; therefore, sin was imputed before the Ten Commandments were written. He said, "How then can I do this great wickedness, and sin against God?" (Genesis 39:9). Remember, where there is no sin, there is no law. Joseph recognized that adultery would be a sin against God, as well as against Mrs. Potiphar, showing that God's Law is an eternal principle—whether or not it is written in stone.

WHICH LAW IS THE LAW

The last sermon of Moses is recorded in Deuteronomy 4:13: "So He declared to you His covenant which He commanded you to perform, that is, the Ten Commandments; and He wrote them on two tablets of stone." God first declared His commands and then wrote them in stone.

A special kind of contract was constructed between God, Moses, and the children of Israel. As with any contract, a verbal agreement was discussed with Moses, and then it was written in the form of a binding contract. God said, "This is my Law. I am the Lord your God that brought you out of the land of Egypt. I love you, and if your love for Me is true you will keep the laws that I have designed for your happiness." After Moses told the people what the Lord had said, they responded, "All that the Lord has said, we will do."

To state it simply, God told His children what He wanted, and they promptly made a promise to obey. Then Moses returned to Mount Sinai where he received the written transcript. Deuteronomy 4:14 continues: "And the Lord commanded me at that time to teach you statutes and judgments, that you might observe them in the land which you cross over to possess." This is a very important Scripture, because the Lord is making a distinction between the Ten Commandments and the other laws, statutes, and judgments.

I don't think it is stretching credibility to think that God considered the Ten Commandments so important that He spoke them with His own voice, while the other laws were delegated to Moses' penmanship. Also, the Commandments were written on stone to represent their eternal endurance, while, in contrast, the ceremonial laws were written on man-made materials. To distinguish them even further, the Ten Commandments were placed inside the Ark of the Covenant, while the other laws were placed in a pocket on the side of the Ark.

We remember these various facts regarding how God gave the laws, wrote the laws, and guarded the laws—it is easy to recognize the difference between the Law of God and the law of Moses. (There will be more about this in the next chapter.)

A LAW FOR ONE NATION

Seventh-day Adventists are often questioned as to why we keep a Jewish Law, because many argue that the Ten Commandments were designed specifically for the Jews. They seem to overlook the fact that God has had a Law from the very beginning of time. Granted, the Law was spoken and then written on Mount Sinai, but it is impossible to suggest that the Law did not exist long before the Sinai event.

The Christian Bible is divided into two sections—the New Testament and the Old Testament. The word *testament* means exactly the same thing as the word *covenant*. Most Christians believe that we are now practicing our faith under the New Covenant. Seventh-day Adventists also believe we are under the New Covenant, but when we talk about obeying God's Law and keeping His Commandments, detractors say, That's the Old Covenant; we're under a New Covenant now.

But is this an accurate analysis? Is it true that the Old Covenant (Old Testament), is for the Jews and the New Covenant (New Testament) is for the Gentiles? Was the New Covenant really made with the Gentiles only? Interestingly, it's the Old Testament that first mentions the New Covenant. In Jeremiah we're told: "'Behold, the days are coming,' says the Lord, 'when I will make a new covenant with the house of Israel and with the house of Judah'" (31:31). The Lord said He will "make a new covenant with the house of Israel." And if that's true, it means that no covenant was specifically made with the Gentiles! The covenant under which all are saved is the same covenant that was made first with the Jews. No wonder the New Testament says that to be saved, one must become Abraham's seed. In other words, we must become "spiritual" Jews.

Some folk really chafe under the concept of becoming a spiritual Jew, indicating that anti-Semitism persists, to some degree, in the Christian church—even while we read a Jewish book and worship a Jewish Savior! According to the Bible, the New Covenant was made with Jews, and to be under that Covenant, one must be either a Jew or a spiritual Jew.

THE PLACE OF THE COVENANTS

Jeremiah 31 speaks more about the New Covenant in the next few verses: "Not according to the covenant that I made with their fathers in the day that I took them by the hand to bring them out of the land of Egypt, My covenant which they broke, though I was a husband to them, says the Lord. But this is the covenant that I will make with the house of Israel" (31:32, 33).

Jeremiah again specified Israel as the house to which His covenant would apply. In verse 33, he continued: "'After those days,' says the Lord, 'I will put My law in their minds, and write it on their hearts.'" Because Jeremiah doesn't specify another law, we must assume it only can be the Ten Commandments!

A BETTER PROMISE

The book of Hebrews also addresses the New Covenant and explains some of the differences between it and the Old Covenant. Hebrews 8:6 teaches: "But now He has obtained a more excellent ministry, inasmuch as He is also Mediator of a better covenant, which was established on better promises."

What is the difference between the New and Old Covenants? *The New Covenant was established on better promises.* So you ask, what was wrong with the Old Covenant?

Remember that the children of Israel promised their Lord, "All that you have said, we will do. We promise you Lord!" However, as the story goes, the children of Israel broke that promise even before Moses descended from the mountain. Unfortunately, the children of Israel were lousy at keeping promises and so are we! Let's look carefully at the differences between the Old and New Covenants as unfolded in the Old and New Testaments.

The Old Covenant was, and remains, an unwieldy combination of the promise of God *and* the not-thought-through promises of people, while the New Covenant rests solely on the promises of God. (That makes it a "better" promise already!) The New Covenant is God's promise of what He is going to do. Can you see the difference? God has said, "I will do it because they have shown they cannot do it." *God still wants us to keep His Laws, but He also knows we cannot do it through our own strength.*

Hebrews 8:7 continues: "For if that first covenant had been faultless, then no place would have been sought for a second." The "fault" with the first law was that people were not able to hold up their end of the bargain. What follows this verse is absolutely critical, because some people argue that the fault lay with the law itself. Verse eight says otherwise: "Because finding fault with them [that is, the Jews], He says: 'Behold, the days are coming, says the Lord, when I will make a new covenant with the house of Israel and with the house of Judah.'"

Understanding that the problem with the Old Covenant was the faulty promises of the people and their inability to keep God's laws through their own strength is imperative.

Hebrews 8 later reviews the very same issues found in Jeremiah 31 regarding the covenants.

We have the same choice today that the Jews had in the Old Testament. Ever since Cain and Abel, we have had a choice to obey God by offering up our best efforts and conforming to external rules, or choosing to obey God by asking for His moment-by-moment "grace to help in time of need" (Hebrews 4:16). The two covenants are like two train tracks running since Cain and Abel, two ways of responding to the Law of God. The two covenants are not two different time periods, (before the Cross and after the Cross), but two ways of trying to please God. One leads to frustration, on the one hand, or to self-satisfaction, on the other; the New Covenant leads to peace, joy, victory—and common sense.

The underlying question is this: Would God create an imperfect law? The Law of the Lord is an expression of His will, and throughout the Bible, it called perfect and just. The book of Romans tells us that God's Law is holy and good (Romans 7:12).

JESUS AND THE LAW

Another argument confronting Adventists is that Jesus came to establish the New Covenant and do away with the law. It is said that He fulfilled the law by living a perfect life. Further, because He "fulfilled" the law we no longer need to obey it. Did He really teach this?

Matthew 5:17 says: "Do not think that I came to destroy the Law or the Prophets. I did not come to destroy but to fulfill." I don't think that Jesus could have made it any clearer! But what about the rest of the verse? It says: "I did not come to destroy, but to fulfill."

The word *fulfill* needs a little explanation. Although we really need to look at the same word in other places in the Bible to let God's Word explain itself, I sometimes like to fit the critic's definition into the verse itself and see if the result is logical. So let's insert *do away* in the place of *fulfill:* "I am not come to destroy [the law], but to [do away with it]." Does that make sense?

Let's look elsewhere in the Bible. In Matthew 3, we read about Jesus being baptized. When John the Baptist saw Jesus in his baptismal procession, he said, "I am the one who needs to be baptized by You, Lord. You are the spotless Lamb of God who takes away the sin of the world." Jesus replied in verse 15: "Permit it to be so now, for thus it is fitting for us to [do away with] all righteousness." Jesus actually used the word *fulfill* where I have inserted *do away with.*

Did Jesus come to abolish or destroy righteousness? The word *fulfill* really means just what it says: to fill something full. Jesus came to magnify the law and make it honorable. He came to prove that the law may be kept through the power of God—a promise that is repeated throughout the New Testament.

As soon as I start talking about the importance of the Law, some say that I'm being legalistic. Was Jesus a legalist when He talked about the law? Setting aside the notion that Jesus quoted the Law when tempted in the wilderness, how did Jesus refer to those who not only kept the law, but taught it to others? He called them the greatest in the kingdom (Matthew 5:19).

In contrast, Jesus makes an equally strong statement pertaining to those who do *not* keep the Law, and encourage others to disobey it. He says that they will be called the "least in the kingdom of God." That means that there will be no room in the kingdom of God for those who willfully disobey the law.

THE LAW OF LOVE

As we have already discovered, many erroneous concepts exist pertaining to the covenants. One interesting challenge to Adventist belief is that the New Covenant is only about love.

Of course, the New Testament has a lot to say about love. John 13:34 says, "A new commandment I give to you, that you love one another; as I have loved you, that you also love one another." But we have to ask ourselves what the Bible is really trying to say about love. Jesus says, "If you love Me, keep my commandments" (John 14:15).

Christ frequently makes this strong connection between obedience and love. However, many Christians worry that when they talk about obedience, this equates to their being legalistic. Yet if obedient Christians are legalistic, that same standard would apply to every Bible writer, as well.

Romans 13:8–10 explains the amazing love story that is lived out in the lives of those who experience the New Covenant: "Owe no one anything except to love one another, for he who loves another has fulfilled the law. For the commandments, 'You shall not commit adultery,' 'You shall not murder,' 'You shall not steal,' 'You shall not bear false witness,' 'You shall not covet,' and if there is any other commandment, are all summed up in this saying, namely, 'You shall love your neighbour as yourself.' Love does no harm to his neighbor; therefore love is the fulfillment of the law."

In other words, Paul says that if you steal, yet say that you love your neighbor, not only are you a thief, but you are a liar as well! 1 John 2:4 says: "He who says, 'I know him,' and does not keep His commandments, is a liar, and the truth is not in him." Those who believe that all Jesus wants from us is our "love" are rejecting one of God's commandments. God doesn't want us to put on a show; if you really love Him, you will be willing to keep His Law (which is really living the life of love).

THE FIRST AND THE GREAT

In Matthew 22:37–40, Jesus said: "You shall love the Lord your God with all your heart, and with all your soul, and with all your mind. This is the first and great commandment. And the second is like it, 'You shall love your neighbor as yourself.' On these two commandments hang all the law and the prophets."

One of the best ways to think about the Ten Commandments is to think about how these verses in Matthew correspond to the Ten Commandments. Simply stated, when you keep the first four commandments, you show your love to the Lord. When you keep the last six commandments, you prove your love for your neighbor.

One by one, compare the individual commandments with "the first and great commandment": If you really love God, you will have no other gods before you. If your whole heart, mind, and soul are devoted to God, nothing will surpass Him in your heart. If you really love God, you will not bow down to graven images. If your heart, mind, and soul are devoted to God, you will not try to pattern Him after a statuette or icon. If you really love God, you will not take His name in vain. If you really love God, you'll want to remember His Sabbath day. (There will be more on this commandment in the next chapter.)

Likewise, the last six commandments must stand the same test. As we saw, Paul outlined this in Romans 13. It's not difficult to grasp that if you love your parents, you will honor them. If you love your neighbor, you will not covet that which is his. And so on.

What it really boils down to is that love is the "fulfillment" of the law! I think we should all admit that the New Covenant is about love and that love is about obedience. It is inaccurate to think that once you have loved, you are at liberty to neglect the Ten Commandments. On the contrary, Paul says that once you have found true love, you will keep God's Law even more carefully.

TWO MISCONCEPTIONS COMPETE WITH THE LAW

One of the more complicated arguments against the Ten Commandments still surprises me. I've heard it expressed this way: "We are not under the law; we are under grace." But what exactly does this mean? This line of reasoning is supposedly based on Romans 6:14, which says: "For sin shall not have dominion over you, for you are not under law, but under grace." I suppose if we all stopped reading here, the argument might sound plausible. But lest anybody misunderstand Paul, he goes on to clarify in the next verse, "What then? Shall we sin, because we are not under the law, but under grace? Certainly not!"

So what does Paul mean by the phrase "under law"? Well, we know that all have sinned and come up short before God's holy and just law. Unless a person accepts Jesus, he or she remains under the curse, the penalty, of the law. But when a person accepts Jesus into the heart as His Lord, Christ frees him from the curse of the law by covering him with His forgiving grace—the blood of the Lamb. Paul, anticipating that somebody might misunderstand this to mean that the forgiven sinner no longer has to keep the law, writes plainly, "Certainly not," ("God forbid," KJV).

A different but related argument that misunderstands Adventists is that we go by the letter of the law, while others go by its spirit. But let's examine this: As an illustration, we know that the Law says we shall not commit adultery. I wonder, is it possible to keep the spirit of the law while breaking the letter? Indeed, in some cases, the spirit of the law is even more difficult; remember when Jesus says that we are not to even look upon a woman with lust in our hearts?

Suppose I say, "I am going to commit adultery, but I will not think about it in my heart." Does that even make sense? No! Instead, the keeping of the spirit of the law always comes after you have at least kept the letter. The letter of the law is the foundation upon which the spirit is built. When someone says she is spiritual because she keeps the spirit of the law and then breaks the letter, she's a liar. John actually calls this kind of person a hypocrite. So you can't say, "I love God," and then break His commandments. It just doesn't make sense.

NOT JUST ADVENTISTS

Of course, it would be false to say that Seventh-day Adventists are the only Christians who believe in the importance of the Law of God.

Dr. Billy Graham was once asked regarding obedience to the Law: "Some religious people I know tell me the Ten Commandments are part of the Law that does not apply to us today. They say that Christians are free from the Law. Is that right?"

Dr. Graham's answer, as quoted in *The Dallas Times Herald*, was, "No, that is not right, and I hope that you will not be misled by these false opinions. It is very important that Christians understand what the Bible means when it says 'free from the law.' It certainly does not mean they are free from the obligations of the moral law of God and that they are at liberty to sin. You see, the word 'law' used in the New Testament is written in two different senses. Sometimes it refers to the ceremonial law of the Old Testament, which is concerned with the ritual matters and regulations of food and drink, etc. This ceremonial law was of a passing character and done away with when Christ came. From this law Christians are indeed free. But the New Testament also speaks of the moral law, which is permanent, unchanging in character, and is summarized in the Ten Commandments. This law sets forth God's demands on human life and man's duty to God. It is quite true that the Christian is not saved by his efforts to keep the law. But as one who is saved by God's mercy through faith in Christ, he is under obligation to obey God's law. It has been said, in Christ we are free from sin, but not free to sin. 'If you love me,' Jesus says, 'keep my commandments.' "

Dr. A. H. Ironside, (radio pastor for the Reformed Church), said, "The law of the Ten Commandments has to do with moral principles and these are of an unchanging nature as any dispensation." Even the Baptist manual has something to say about the Law of God. "We believe the scriptures teach that the law of God is the eternal, unchanging rule of His moral government that is holy, just and good. Unfeigned obedience to the Holy Law is the end objective of the gospel. The Lord wants to save us from sin and sin is the transgression of God's law."

THE DEVIL AND THE LAW

Why does the devil hate the Law? It's really very simple—by the Law is the knowledge of sin. James very appropriately compares the Law to a mirror. When we see God's Law, we become aware of our sinfulness and our need for God to cleanse our hearts.

The Law creates within us not only a desire for forgiveness, but also a desire to live closer to our Savior. When the devil attacks the Law of God, he is attempting to sabotage the motivating forces that bring us to Jesus.

He knows quite well that the Law leads us to Christ. The Law helps us to identify that we are sinners, but it does not save us. Our salvation lies solely in Christ's forgiving and empowering grace.

I once presented a week of prayer in a packed prison chapel. One inmate told me that he had been a Seventh-day Adventist, but had wandered from the church. He had been told that the Law did not matter. Now he will be spending the rest of his life behind bars for murder. It's fascinating to preach to prisoners; they have no trouble comprehending that God wants our obedience. They are so grateful for salvation from disobedience. They believe that God gives them power to be different people.

I hope I never hear of a Christian minister walking into a prison and telling people they are no longer under the Law. Every prisoner of sin needs to hear that Christ will give him or her the power to do His will. But who could ever feel safe in today's society if the laws of the land were suddenly eliminated?

If you feel reluctant to reintroduce into your community men and women who have not learned to obey the laws of the land, imagine God introducing into heaven those who have not had a change of heart—people who don't want to obey the Ten Commandments? Jesus says that not all professed Christians will enter into His gates, but only those that have done the will of His Father. Obedience is truly the highest form of love. The new earth will surely be filled with "law-abiding" people saved by grace from this sin-sick world.

THE LAW OF HEAVEN

Let's take this concept one step further. Matthew 5:18 says: "For assuredly, I say to you, till heaven and earth pass away, one jot or one tittle will by no means pass from the law till all is fulfilled." I do believe that there will be a day again when we will not need the written Law. When we are filled with love in the new earth, I don't think that we will be toting the Ten Commandments over our shoulders to make sure that we are behaving obediently. Instead, obedience will be the natural response of a loving heart toward God and our fellow man. "Whosoever therefore breaks one of the least of these commandments, and teaches men so, shall be called least in the kingdom of heaven; but whoever does and teaches them, he shall be called great in the kingdom of heaven" (Matthew 5:19).

Does obedience in heaven mean legalism? Should it mean that here today? For example, before my son Stephen leaves for school in the morning, I always hear my wife, Karen, ask, "Stephen, has your bed been made?" What if he started to answer back, "Aw, Mom, you're legalistic." Even at his young age, he understands that his parents lovingly require obedience and that he has to make his bed before he leaves for school. He makes his best effort to straighten his sheets and blankets, but sometimes it looks to me like he did it with an eggbeater. As his parents, we accept his well-intended efforts as we teach him. Am I a legalistic parent because I expect his obedience? I don't think so.

It is time to take a stand for God and to allow His Law to make a change in your life in dramatic fashion. Others may tell you that you are legalistic as you demonstrate your obedience to God, but don't feel ashamed!

Many people in the world feel timid about addressing the importance of God's Law, because they fear being labeled a legalist. But you should never feel embarrassed by being loyal to God. Make certain, however, that you always couple a presentation of the law with the appropriate story of grace. *Otherwise you are a legalist!*

I cannot deny that there are legalists in the Seventh-day Adventist church, as surely as there are legalists in the Baptist and Catholic faiths. Every denomination contains people who have not seen the difference between the Old and New Covenant experiences. But we all can accept Paul's appeal to understand experientially the joy of "obedience to the faith" (Romans 1:5; 16:26).

Chapter Two

ADVENTISTS AND THE SABBATH

The best doctrine, and one of the most criticized, of the Seventh-day Adventist church is the seventh-day Sabbath. It's part of our name, and thus one of the central pillars of our belief system.

Seventh-day Adventists spend a lot of time talking about the Sabbath. We recognize that the fourth commandment says that if we love God with all our heart, we will remember His Sabbath. In fact, being obedient to this law is the epitome of showing our loyalty and love to God.

Practically speaking, it's not much different than your relationship with your spouse. If you love your lifelong mate, you enjoy being with him or her! How many have heard the pitch, "Spend quality time together"? Every love relationship revolves around quality time.

Thus the Sabbath represents uninterrupted quality time with our Maker, thinking the thoughts He wants us to think and doing the things He enjoys doing with us. This time is strictly for worshipping and abiding in His presence. Will this day be important to you if you truly love God and want to do whatever He says? Of course! But sadly, the devil uses many avenues to attack the Sabbath because he knows that this is one of the most important times when we nurture our love relationship with God.

PROTESTING THE SABBATH

In his book *Weighed and Found Wanting*, Dwight L. Moody, a mighty preacher of the nineteenth century, recorded his thoughts about God's law: "The commandments of God given to Moses on the Mount at Horeb are as binding today as they have ever been since the time that they were proclaimed in the hearing of the people. The people must be made to understand the Ten Commandments are still as binding and that there is a penalty attached to their violation." Moody regarded the fourth commandment this way: "I honestly believe that this commandment is just as binding today as it ever was. I have talked with men who have said it was abrogated, but they have never been able to point to any place in the Bible where God repealed it. When Christ was on earth He did nothing to set it aside."

Yet while Protestant America soundly declares the glory of God's law and the absolute surety of His Word, they find the fourth commandment very troublesome.

Once, before holding a series of evangelistic meetings, I visited a local church on Sunday. An attractive display of the Ten Commandments was hanging on the wall. It so happened that Sunday service was dedicated to a study of the Commandments. The minister looked my way, and I knew he recognized me as being a Seventh-day Adventist pastor.

The preacher covered each of the Ten Commandments in the order in which they are recorded. It was with careful delicacy that he approached the fourth commandment, saying, "And make sure you remember the Sabbath each week." He certainly was not about to specify which day that was, because there, for all to see, the commandment said it for him—the seventh day.

ONE FOR ALL, ALL FOR ONE

When my evangelistic series began, that preacher and several of his church members attended. When the issue of the Sabbath was inevitably raised, he tried to poke holes in the theory using several of the arguments we discussed in the last chapter. He said, "We are not under the law anymore, we are under grace." Amazingly, with that statement, he went back to his church and promptly removed the Ten Commandments from the wall.

Furthermore, the children of his congregation had a lesson in their Sunday school class about the Ten Commandments, but their teacher took away their lesson guides, with this justification, "The Ten Commandments are legalistic! We cannot teach this any longer to our children."

Over the years, several Protestant churches have realized that if they are going to teach the law to their congregations, consistency is necessary. Unfortunately, because there are not many churches that can consistently teach the Ten Commandments, many have stopped teaching them altogether.

I often wonder if this awkwardness and inconsistency is partly to blame for the accelerating crime in our communities. Our culture needs to understand the law of God now more than ever, but there is this ironic misguided fear that if you are going to teach the law, you had better teach it all—including the Sabbath. Most Christians are not sure whether they should accept the impact that this law might have in their lives.

CONTROVERSIAL FOR A REASON

The Sabbath has been a topic of contention and a cause of dissension for centuries, and it continues to cause a stir among spiritual leaders and lay people of all denominations. Yet we know from the Bible that the history of the Sabbath goes back to the very beginning of earth's history. So what happened to the seventh-day Sabbath that once announced the birthday of life on Planet Earth?

Could it really be that the Sabbath has since been altered from the seventh day to the first day of the week? Could it have been abolished entirely? Thankfully, God has not left us to wrestle with these questions alone. With laser precision He has kept the light of truth on His own special day. With His own voice, He clearly gave His earthly children the very same legal principles that govern heaven, and with His finger He chiseled them into a tablet of stone.

The Ten Commandments were given to us as laws of love intended to guide us in our yearning for human happiness. As a result, the civil laws of most civilized governments in some way resemble many of the Ten Commandments. The first three commandments, which address our relationship to God, are readily embraced by most Christians. What Christian won't agree that we should respect God's name or shun idolatry? Yet many stumble over the Sabbath commandment, making it a source of disruption in the God-man relationship that the Ten Commandments were meant to establish.

I find it ironic that the one commandment that asks us to "remember" is the one that most people try to forget. The fourth commandment is very special in that it affects us all—every seventh day around the world it calls out to be remembered. God seeks to nurture our fellowship and devotion by teaching us to remember the Sabbath. So why are Protestants still protesting it?

IS THE SEVENTH DAY STILL THE SEVENTH DAY?

The Sabbath is clearly important to God. He placed it in the middle of the Ten Commandments, saying, "Remember the Sabbath day, to keep it holy. Six days you shall labor, and do all your work, but the seventh day is the Sabbath of the Lord your God." Does it matter, then, which day we observe the Sabbath?

Let's establish a basic fact before going on to the more serious arguments. If you open up your dictionary and look up the word "Saturday," it's going to tell you, "Saturday is the seventh day of the week." You can also look up the word "Sunday" and find that it is defined as the first day of the week. That is about as basic a proof available, and most calendars say the week begins with Sunday, the first day, and ends with Saturday, the seventh day.

One argument that is used against Seventh-day Adventists is that the calendar has been changed, or adjusted, so that we cannot know which day is the Sabbath. It's true that the calendar has been modified—several times actually. However, these changes have never affected the days of the week. Indeed, the seven-day, weekly cycle is distinct from the solar calendar year that has needed adjustments through the centuries.

Most countries today follow the Gregorian calendar. In 1582, Pope Gregory changed October 5 to October 15 in just one day. What was Friday, October 5, became Friday, October 15. The days of the week were unchanged. The purpose of this change was to make the seasons more consistent, and it also created the need for our leap year because we fall back a day every four years. (Leap year also doesn't affect the weekly cycle!)

Of course, the notion that the calendar change transformed the weekly cycle really doesn't make sense. Saturday has been the seventh day since creation and continues to be the seventh day today. The U.S. Naval Observatory substantiates this with historical events that have been mapped using astronomy.

The Bible also tells us that Jesus died on the preparation day, before the Sabbath began, and rose on the first day, after the Sabbath ended (Luke 23:54–24:1). He kept the Sabbath even in His death, and He rose on Sunday not to rest, but to begin His High Priestly ministry.

Thus, the seventh-day Sabbath can be supported by the dictionary, the encyclopedia, the Bible, and just plain common sense.

HOW CAN SO MANY PEOPLE BE WRONG?

If Saturday is indeed the seventh day, then why are there so many Christians who do not recognize Saturday as the Sabbath? At one time, I was a Christian who worshipped on Sunday. Even though I am half Jewish, I knew nothing about the seventh-day Sabbath. When I learned about the Sabbath, I remember thinking, "How could so many people be wrong, or so few be so right?" But today I know that's not a defense, because all you have to do is read the Bible to understand that there is a pattern in which "only a handful" happens over and over again.

Did the majority of God's people recognize Jesus when He was born in a stable? Did the religious leaders, with all their diplomas, know who He was? It was only a handful of shepherds and fishermen who recognized Him. It was not the majority who believed in the long-awaited Messiah.

I began visiting different pastors at the church where I worshipped, searching for an answer to this question. Their confusing and incompatible answers eventually helped lead me to believe that Saturday was God's day of rest for man.

I was told, "Well, Doug, yes. We're to keep the Ten Commandments, but Sunday is now the Sabbath." When I asked one pastor why, he said, "Because Jesus rose on the first day of the week, and that is now the new Sabbath for Christians." But wherever you look in the Bible, this claim can not be substantiated.

From another minister I heard, "We aren't under the law anymore." But when I asked if one could break any of the Ten Commandments, he said, "Of course not! We keep the other nine." The more I studied, the more evidence I gathered. The more I gathered, the less I could escape the glaring truth that the seventh day is most definitely still the Sabbath, and we are still commanded to keep it.

Ultimately, it became clear to me that it boiled down to a long-standing tradition in our churches that Sunday is kept as the Sabbath. Nothing is wrong with tradition essentially, of course. Tradition counts for something. But Jesus did say, "Why do you set aside the Commandments of God that you might observe tradition?"

STONE AND ETERNITY

The idea that God etched His laws into stone with His finger says a lot. It symbolizes that the Ten Commandments are eternal, forever unchanging. Malachi says, "I am the Lord God, I change not." God is not wishy-washy in His decisions. It was not by mistake that He gave a law or chose the seventh day to be the Sabbath.

In Matthew 24:20, Jesus warned: "And pray that your flight may not be in the winter, or on the sabbath day." Why would Jesus say something like that? Some explain that this is because the gates of Jerusalem were shut on the Sabbath day, and they were to pray that they would not be locked inside. But that doesn't make sense in light of the winter reference. The more plausible idea is that these Jews would be forced to flee to the mountains, and Jesus knew that it would be difficult to keep the Sabbath sacred if you were fleeing for your life. He also understood that it would not be wise to flee during the winter because there would be no crops in the fields to sustain the refugees.

In Genesis 2:1–3, the seventh-day Sabbath is described (before sin occurred) as part of God's perfect plan in Paradise. He blessed it, hallowed it, and set it aside as a special day of worship and communion between God and man. Adam and Eve were the only two people on earth when God declared that the Sabbath was made for humanity. Notice He did not say that the Sabbath was made only for Jews. The Sabbath is not a Jewish law. It is for the entire human race, because every single one of us not only needs physical rest, we need that holy time to worship our Creator.

Thus from Genesis to Revelation, the Bible is full of the seventh-day Sabbath. Isaiah 66:22, 23 speaks of heaven and the new earth, saying: "'For as the new heavens and the new earth which I will make shall remain before Me,' says the LORD, 'so shall your descendants and your name remain. And it shall come to pass, that from one New Moon to another, and from one Sabbath to another, all flesh shall come to worship before Me,' says the Lord." In the new earth, all flesh will worship God on the Sabbath.

Additionally, when Paul preached on the Sabbath, he spoke to both Jews and Gentiles (see Acts 17:1–4; 18:1–4; 20:21). Paul knew what to do on the seventh day: "And on the Sabbath we went out of the city to the riverside, where prayer was customarily made; and we sat down, and spoke to the women who met there" (Acts 16:13).

Paul was a tent maker by trade and the Bible speaks of him praying and preaching on the Sabbath day, but it never mentions him making tents on Sabbath. Revelation 22:14 says, "Blessed are those who do his commandments, that they may have the right to the tree of life, and may enter in through the gates into the city."

THE SABBATH AND THE RESURRECTION

I have often heard the argument that the Sabbath was changed to Sunday in the New Testament. But are you aware that in the New Testament, neither Saturday nor Sunday is mentioned directly, although they are both referred to?

Because Saturday, Sunday, Monday, etc., are Roman names, they are not found in the Bible. Rather, the days of the week are noted as the first, second, third, fourth, fifth, preparation, and Sabbath day. Anytime you see "first day" in the Bible, you will never see it referred to as the new Sabbath. There's never even a hint of it. God didn't make a mistake with His law.

The first reference to the "first day" in the New Testament can be found in Matthew 28:1. As with most of the following verses, this text deals primarily with the day that Jesus rose from the tomb. Of course Jesus rose on the first day of the week. He also died on Friday—but does that make Friday or Sunday a new Sabbath day? What day of the week was the Last Supper? It took place on the evening before Jesus died, or Thursday. Does that make Thursday a new holy day? Christ did wonderful things on many different days of the week, but that does not transform any one of them into a new Sabbath.

Matthew also said, "Now after the Sabbath, as the first day of the week began to dawn, Mary Magdalene and the other Mary came to see the tomb." This verse outlines the days very clearly, but even clearer was the disciples' attitude toward caring for Jesus' body on the Sabbath. Luke spoke of how the disciples did not finish anointing His body as Friday evening arrived, because they did not wish to violate the Sabbath.

If Jesus taught that the Sabbath no longer mattered, then why were the disciples so sensitive about it that they would not finish embalming their dead leader until the day after? Mark 16:2 records: "Very early in the morning, on the first day of the week, they came to the tomb when the sun had risen." We know, of course, that Jesus had already risen, leaving only a neat pile of burial clothes behind. Yet does Mark here mention a substitute day for the Sabbath? Mark 16:9 also refers to the first day, stating: "Now when He rose early on the first day of the week, He appeared first to Mary Magdalene, out of whom He had cast seven devils." But there is still no mention of a Sabbath switch.

Luke referenced the first day again in 24:1: "Now on the first day of the week, very early in the morning, they, and certain other women with them, came to the tomb, bringing the spices which they had prepared." Still no mention of a new Sabbath.

John 20:1,19 says: "On the first day of the week Mary Magdalene came to the tomb early, while it was still dark, and saw that the stone had been taken away from the tomb ... Then, the same day at evening, being the first day of the week, when the doors were shut where the disciples were assembled for fear of the Jews." Why did the disciples assemble together? Was it to inaugurate a new Sabbath day? No! The Bible very clearly states they gathered togethe· in fear of the Jews.

THE SABBATH AND THE EARLY CHURCH

If the Sabbath was that important to the disciples, how do we get the idea that the Sabbath is no longer important today? Since Jesus never mentioned a change and His disciples kept the Sabbath even after His death, we need to look at the early church for evidence.

One tricky Scripture that is used to cite a change in the Sabbath is Acts 20:7, which reports: "Now on the first day of the week, when the disciples came together to break bread, Paul, ready to depart the next day, spoke to them, and continued his message until midnight." It is argued that this verse is referring to a communion service on Sunday, because it's clear the disciples are breaking bread on the first day. However, this is really a leap of logic, since Jesus and His disciples broke bread together on many different days of the week. Breaking bread does not always symbolize communion; sometimes it simply means to eat together.

As the story goes, Paul preached at this dinner for so long that a man in the audience fell asleep and tumbled from the third-loft window and died! Paul embraced the man and

prayed, and Scripture says the man was resurrected. Are we
told this story because God wants us to know that He has
inaugurated another Sabbath day? (Or perhaps it is just a
lesson reminding preachers to end their sermons before
somebody dies!)

After the man was raised from the dead, the gathering
headed upstairs to break bread again. In the Bible, days
begin and end at sundown. This farewell gathering actually
began on what we would today call Saturday night, but in
Bible language it was the beginning of the first day of the
week. As the Sabbath sun settled into the horizon, Sunday
began. So technically all of the exciting events of the evening
took place on what we call Saturday night.

The next several verses report on Paul's travels, which
began early the next morning. If the Sabbath had been
changed to Sunday, would we really expect a good Sabbath-
keeper like Paul to devote his day to traveling? Absolutely
not! No Sabbath-keeper would begin a tough day of travel
on the Sabbath.

The last Scripture in the New Testament that makes
any specific reference to the first day, Sunday, is
1 Corinthians 16:2: "On the first day of the week let each of
you lay something aside, as he may prosper, that there be no
collections when I come." Some of those who argue against
Adventists point to this verse as a clincher, because they say
that it describes the taking of a collection or offering during
a church service. Actually, that's a stretch because it literally
means the very opposite. Paul is saying, "Let each person
set aside at the beginning of the week that which God has
prospered him with."

In the Sabbath-keeping economy in which these Jews
and Christians participated, the tithes and offerings were
brought on Sabbath, and then the next day—the first day
of the week—the members got their accounts in order in
preparation for the next Sabbath's tithes and offerings. If

they had extra funds, it would be given to the starving saints in Jerusalem. In essence, Paul was taking up an emergency relief-fund offering for the disadvantaged. He said, "In order that there be no offerings during our regular services, lay by you at your house in store when I come." This was the system of church charity in that day.

THE PROBLEM WITH CHANGING A PERFECT LAW

Neither in the Old nor New Testaments have we seen even one example of the Sabbath being changed to Sunday. In reality, the record of the Sabbath change is found long after the days of Peter, James, and John and the resurrection of Christ. In fact, many years later this almost imperceptible shift filtered through Christianity.

To cross the heathen divide and reach the Roman pagans, some Christians began to embrace the day of the sun, otherwise known as Sunday, along with Roman culture. For a while, some Christians kept both Saturday and Sunday, but gradually for most of Christianity, creeping compromise eventually allowed Sunday to substitute for the seventh day. (The Bible warns that serving two masters ultimately leads to disobedience.)

This information about the change from Saturday to Sunday can be found in almost any encyclopedia. Where the Sunday Sabbath came from is no secret. You can read about it in history books and Catholic catechisms. Bible scholars of every persuasion will agree that there is absolutely no biblical support for changing the Sabbath, and almost all will agree that the change came about as a result of self appointed church authority.

Now that we have settled the question of whether the Sabbath was changed in the Bible, we must address the question of whether the Sabbath has been abolished altogether. Did faith, or grace, or the Holy Spirit change it? As we have already seen, we have no biblical record of any change in the Sabbath commandment or any other of the Ten.

But let's revisit last chapter's brief discussion of the two different sets of laws spoken of in the Bible. The Ten Commandments are a concise and separate set of precepts that stand apart from all other laws—they are often called "the Law." The Bible also uses the term "law" to refer to other kinds of law. Sometimes the word "law" is used to describe the first five books of the Old Testament, while at other times it is used to describe the civil and health laws of the Jewish nation. The tendency of some Bible students to loosely use the term "law" to describe all the laws in the Bible, including the Ten Commandments and the ceremonial law, has been used by Sabbath critics to create a compelling argument against the Sabbath. They claim that the Sabbath law was "nailed to the cross," along with the ceremonial laws (Colossians 2:14). But this ultimately doesn't work, because the Bible distinguishes the moral law from the ceremonial laws.

But the question lingers: Is it really possible that there are laws in the Bible that Christians today are not obligated to keep? For instance, does the Bible require Christian males to be circumcised? Paul answers this question in 1 Corinthians 7:19: "Circumcision is nothing, and uncircumcision is nothing, but keeping the commandments of God is what matters." In other words, Paul says that the ceremonial laws, including circumcision, are not the things that matter.

Yet in Romans 3:31, Paul writes: "Do we then make void the law through faith? Certainly not! On the contrary, we establish the law." Here we see that keeping the commandments of God is imperative for Christians! What commandments? The Ten Commandments. Paul is saying, in so many words, that it doesn't make sense to say we don't need to keep the Sabbath because we now live by faith: "What shall we say then? Shall we continue in sin, that grace may abound? Certainly not! How shall we who died to sin live any longer in it?" (Romans 6:1).

Still, the argument goes that Paul has also said: "For sin shall not have dominion over you, for you are not under the law, but under grace" (Romans 6:14). What did Paul mean? Are we no longer obligated to keep the law, even as he already has pleaded, "Certainly not!" ("God forbid!" KJV.) No, he means that we are not under the penalty of the law, because of God's grace!

Three times Paul talks about the relationship between the law, grace, and faith. Three times he repeats it, lest people mistakenly conclude that he is giving Christians liberty to disobey the law. In other words, what part of "Certainly not!" and "God forbid!" don't we understand?

SPIRIT OF DISOBEDIENCE

So, if we have not been freed from the law by faith or by grace, perhaps we can find liberty from the law through the spirit, some suggest. Romans 7:6 says: "But now we have been delivered from the law, having died to what we were held by, so that we should serve in the newness of the Spirit, and not in the oldness of the letter." With that verse in mind, I've been told, "Doug, don't worry about the Sabbath anymore because you are under the Spirit. Otherwise, you're just following the letter of the law."

Of course, this argument is saying that the spirit of the law does not require a strict adherence to the fourth commandment. But that creates a stunning contradiction once you apply that principle to the other nine commandments! Have you ever considered saying, "I keep the spirit of the law that says you're not to commit adultery. I do cheat on my husband now and then but spiritually I keep the law." Try that on stealing or lying!

As we discussed in the previous chapter, it's impossible to keep the spirit of the law while breaking the letter of the law. Yet when it comes to the fourth commandment, people say: "I don't keep the Sabbath literally but I do keep it spiritually." But would you buy it if your child said, "I didn't eat my mashed potatoes, but spiritually they're all gone."

Could Paul say it any clearer: "For not the hearers of the law are just in the sight of God, but the doers of the law will be justified" (Romans 2:13). We're not only obligated to *hear* the law, we must also become *doers* of the law through faith in God and His grace.

Esteeming One Day Above Another

Another argument used to counter Adventism is found in Romans 14:5: "One person esteems one day above another; another esteems every day alike." Many declare that according to this verse, Paul is saying that the seventh-day Sabbath is no longer a Christian requirement. But Paul continued, "Let each be fully persuaded in his own mind. He who observes the day observes it to the Lord; and he that does not observe the day, to the Lord he does not observe it."

What is going on here? Is the Lord really vacillating between what He said and what *we* take Him to mean? Indeed, is it appropriate to think that He would have people stoned at one time for disobeying His law, especially the fourth commandment, then later suggest we can worship Him according to our own standards? Not at all! Paul is talking about the Jewish ceremonial laws, as one can see from the context of chapter 14. The ceremonial law had a number of "sabbath" days that were distinct from the seventh-day Sabbath of the Ten Commandments—the Sabbath that existed before sin was committed in the Garden of Eden. The ceremonial Sabbath days, such as Passover, the Feast of the Tabernacles, and the Feast of the Trumpets, were added later as part of the plan of salvation, to help deal with the sin problem. Remember, these ceremonial commandments were written on man-made materials rather than on stone and spoken by Moses rather than God.

So in Romans 14:5, 6, Paul is dealing with Jewish holidays, or sabbaths, that originated from the earlier ceremonial law. Paul was saying that if you are going to observe them, observe them to the Lord. For instance, if a member of my congregation felt strongly that a special service be held to remember the resurrection of the Lord that took place around the Easter holiday, I would say, "If you want to regard the day, do it to the Lord, but not for the Easter bunnies."

To use Paul's writing here to excuse Christians from seventh-day Sabbath-keeping is to purposefully deny that he's talking about ceremonial laws. How do we know? Because he also writes in Colossians 2:14–17: "Having wiped out the handwriting of requirements that was against us, which was contrary to us. And He has taken it out of the way, having nailed it to the cross … Let no one judge you … regarding … sabbaths, which are a shadow of things to come; but the substance is of Christ."

Similarly, others use Galatians to suggest that we are not under the law—that the law is bondage. But Galatians does not even mention the Sabbath. The closest mention is in Galatians 4:10, 11: "You observe days and months and seasons and years. I am afraid for you, lest I have labored for you in vain." By this Paul was referring, again, to the Jewish holidays—the dates, the seasons and the years. He is not talking about the seventh-day Sabbath.

After sin entered the world, the Lord established holy days, such as the Passover, to help Jews look forward to the coming Savior. The Passover was a "shadow" of things to come. After Jesus came, Christians could see more clearly what the blood on the door post meant to those Israelites ready to leave Egypt. Christ's life and death would become the blood over the door of our hearts, guaranteeing that sinners saved by grace would not have to pay the wages for their sin—which is death. The Sabbath in Creation was not a shadow—it was part of God's master plan. Paul says, "Do not let anyone judge you regarding those sabbath days which are shadows," that is, holy days pertaining to the ceremonial law. Keep your eyes on the big picture, and the purpose for remembering the seventh-day Sabbath: "to keep it holy."

THE LAW OF BONDAGE?

In James 2, we find the Ten Commandments (which includes the seventh-day Sabbath) referred to as the law of liberty, while the ceremonial law is called a law contained in ordinances. Once again, the moral law was written by God's finger on a stone tablet, while the ceremonial laws were written by Moses on man-made materials. Likewise, the Ten Commandments were placed in the Ark of the Covenant, while the other laws were placed on the outside. The moral law is eternal, but the ceremonial law ended at the cross.

So much of the ceremonial law dealt with sacrifices and blood; their purpose was fulfilled when Christ became the ultimate sacrificial lamb. The ceremonial law served its purpose, but the Bible tells us that the purpose of the Sabbath will never end. Will it be necessary to sacrifice an innocent lamb in heaven? No. Will we gather before the Lord on the Sabbath in heaven? Absolutely. The Sabbath will be honored in heaven, just as God's universe will always honor the other nine laws of liberty.

I'm amazed that most Christians, both Protestant and Catholic, have no problem accepting the Ten Commandments until it is time to talk about the Sabbath. But it remains a difficult task to take the Fourth Commandment out of the Ten

Commandment Law. It seems ludicrous to say, "Remember them all except the one that says 'remember.'"

Others use the argument that only the important commandments have been repeated in the New Testament. They are right! Nine commandments are explicitly listed in the New Testament, including the fourth commandment. The one that is not specifically listed, but is clearly alluded to, is the third.

Nowhere in the New Testament will you find the commandment: "Thou shalt not take the name of the Lord thy God in vain; for the Lord will not hold him guiltless that taketh his name in vain." The Lord's Prayer says, "Hallowed be Thy name," addressing the *principle* in the New Testament, while not actually quoting the commandment. Is it acceptable then to take the Lord's name in vain? The arguments used to refute the Sabbath are contradictory, feeble, and sometimes even desperate.

The early Christians did question specific issues, but the Sabbath was not one of them. They understood the basic Ten Commandments, but often had trouble understanding how to practically incorporate biblical principles into their lifestyles. They were concerned about food that had been offered to idols and co-habitation taking place outside of marriage. Accordingly, Paul addressed these specific issues.

In Acts 15:10, Paul said: "Now therefore, why do you test God by putting a yoke on the neck of the disciples which neither our fathers nor we were able to bear?" Verse 24 continues: "Since we have heard that some who went out from us have troubled you with words, unsettling your souls, saying, 'You must be circumcised and keep the law'—to whom we gave no such commandment." Which law is he speaking of? Paul is speaking of the ceremonial laws.

AN EXODUS FROM SLAVERY

Exodus 4 dramatically tells the story of the bondage the children of Israel experienced under Egyptian captivity. The people were weary and demoralized by the time God established Moses as their leader. However, despite their low morale, the time had come for God to deliver His people.

As Moses and Aaron met with the elders of Israel, they "bowed their heads and worshipped" as they rededicated their lives to God before this great task. They left that small gathering encouraged that the Lord was about to do something great for the people of Israel. With that in mind, Aaron and Moses stood before the courts of Pharaoh and boldly declared, "Thus says the Lord God of Israel: 'Let my people go.'"

The Israelite population had grown considerably, and this enslaved community contributed greatly to Pharaoh's wealth. He had no intention of allowing them freedom. He said in Exodus 5:5: "Look, the people of the land are many now, and you make them rest from their labor." The Hebrew word for "rest" used here is "shabath." In other words, Moses was causing the children of Israel to honor the Sabbath.

During the centuries of slavery, the Israelites had come to neglect the Sabbath. However, it is also clear that the Sabbath was reintroduced as the people re-dedicated their lives to God in preparation for their exit from the land of Egypt. It was unfortunate that in response to Moses' demand, Pharaoh declared: "Let more work be laid on them for they think they have time to gather together for a few days to worship their God. Let them find their own straw but make them keep their old quotas!"

Jesus was chosen to liberate us from the bondage of sin just as Moses was God's instrument to deliver the Israelites from slavery. Consequently, Satan responds similarly to Pharaoh as he strives to keep God's people too busy and distracted from the Sabbath. The workloads are increased and the demands for our time become more fervent. Meanwhile, a frazzled society craves a day of rest but fears that they just do not have enough time to take off and worship.

NOT A SABBATH OF CULTS

Walter Martin, in his book *The Kingdom of the Cults*, struggled to explain why Seventh-day Adventists are committed to the seventh-day Sabbath. He finally says, "They are saying that they are saved by grace and yet they are trying to keep the Commandments." Walter Martin thus misunderstood the reason why Seventh-day Adventists strive to honor the Ten Commandments. We do not keep them in order to be *saved,* we keep them because we are *already* abiding in Jesus. Jesus said, "If you love me, keep my Commandments." We keep the Sabbath because our hearts are turned toward Him in love.

Believing that the Sabbath does not matter to God is a very dangerous position to take. Throughout the Bible, we find evidence for the seventh-day Sabbath, beginning with creation and ending with the promise of keeping the Sabbath in the New Earth (Isaiah 66:23).

If in doubt, we should live as Christ lived. Did Jesus heal on the Sabbath? Yes! Did Jesus feed the hungry on the Sabbath? Yes! Did Jesus worship with others on the Sabbath? Yes! Christ taught, "It is better to do good on the Sabbath day." Included in all that He came to accomplish, Jesus came to liberate the Sabbath from the cumbersome, man-made traditions that the Jewish leaders had attached to this day of rest. The Sabbath is a day for doing good. It is not to be a burden, but a blessing to every living soul (Isaiah 58:13, 14).

"For this is the love of God, that we keep his commandments: and his commandments are not grievous" (1 John 5:3). Jesus said, "Take my yoke upon you, and I will give you rest." Just as Pharaoh did to the Israelites, Satan today would like nothing more than to see you "making bricks without straw" so that you will have no time to spend remembering your Creator and His promises to make your life abundant with joy. If you have chosen to be saved by God then you must know Him. The only way to know and love God is to spend quality time with Him. That's why He gave the seventh-day Sabbath to the human race.

When you spend that quality time in communion with Him every seventh day, you will know that He loved you enough to take away your burdens at the high cost of His life. Remembering the Sabbath day to keep it holy is God's gift to you. Far from being a burden, the Sabbath will become a burden-lifter, and the longer you honor it, the more you will prize it as the time when God comes especially close to everyone in this wide world.

Chapter Three

ADVENTISTS AND ELLEN WHITE

Seventh-day Adventism is not just like other Protestant churches. It should be obvious that several of our foundational beliefs don't mesh with those of other churches. One of the most prominent distinctives of the Seventh-day Adventist church will be discussed in this chapter.

Next to the Sabbath and the charge of legalism, the place of Ellen White in the Adventist Church is probably the most common source of misunderstanding. I want to discuss this with you using the sound teachings of the Bible.

This particular doctrinal emphasis leads many people to classify the church as a cult. They wonder, "How could a woman who was hit in the head with a brick not have visions! She was probably just hallucinating."

I was listening to a Bible talk radio program when a caller asked about the seventh-day Sabbath in relation to Seventh-day Adventists. The host, who fancies himself a Bible scholar, said, "Well, Seventh-day Adventists believe in the Sabbath because during a vision their prophet, Ellen White, saw a halo around the seventh day." I wanted so badly to call him and help him out of his ignorance! Among this and other misconceptions, Ellen White and her prolific writings are constantly under attack. But what is the truth about her and her role in the Seventh-day Adventist church?

THE BIBLE AND THE PROPHETS

People fear what they do not understand. Perhaps this explains why many gross misunderstandings exist regarding

Ellen White's role in the Seventh-day Adventist church. Indeed, I have often asked some of the loudest objectors of Ellen White if they have ever read any of her writings. Most often the answer is, "Well, no. My church does not allow it," or "No, I wouldn't want to be hypnotized or brainwashed like you are."

But talking like that without even the smallest education regarding Ellen White's writings is potentially disastrous. I want to begin by establishing that in Scripture, God always worked through Spirit-filled people before doing anything significant in history. For instance, Noah was a prophet who foretold the future, predicting the great flood that God told him was coming. Moses was a prophet whom God used to bring the children of Israel out of Egyptian slavery. Isaiah and Jeremiah were both extraordinary prophets used to warn their nation of impending disaster. Not every prophet has shared the same job description, however. John the Baptist was a prophet whose job was to pave the way for Christ's mission on earth. But as you look through the Bible, you will see that, one way or another, before God does something significant, He sends messengers to prepare, warn, and lead His people.

The plan of salvation began with the birth of Christ and will climax with His glorious Second Coming. As Jesus predicted, we are now living in a time when the world is plunged into confusion and distraction. With the earth on the verge of such a great time of trouble, and with the return of Jesus imminent, is it so difficult to believe that the Lord would step in and speak through an end-time messenger?

The Bible answers this question for us. Joel 2:28-29 and Acts 2:17 record: "And it shall come to pass afterward, that I will pour out My Spirit on all flesh; Your sons and your daughters shall prophesy, Your old men shall dream dreams, Your young men shall see visions; And also on My manservants and upon My maidservants I will pour out My Spirit in those days." God will pour out His Spirit in the form of gifts upon certain individuals in the last days. Could prophecy be one of those gifts?

Yet some still believe that the days of the prophets ended in the Old Testament. However, 1 Corinthians 12:28 says: "And God has appointed these in the church, first apostles, second prophets, third teachers, after that miracles, then gifts of healings, helps, administrations, varieties of tongues." Are we still in the days of the church? We might not have 12 apostles any longer, but consider that one of the primary roles of the apostles was to act as spiritual administrators and leaders in the church. And godly servants still act in this capacity today.

According to Paul, God has also placed prophets in the church, counting it as the second prominent gift to the church. Of course, he also adds teachers, miracle workers, gifts of healing, helps, administrations, and a variety of tongues.

I strongly believe that every one of these gifts is still available to the church today.

The history of the church shows a strong cyclical pattern to the distribution of "gifts." Even in the Old Testament, gifts came at crucial times and in different ways. Consider the story of Gideon in the book of Judges. When an angel appeared to him and said the Lord would be with him as he led Israel out of their bondage, Gideon, perhaps confused, basically answered, "How can you say that the Lord will be with us? Whatever happened to the miracles and signs and wonders that we saw in the old days, back when the children of Israel were led out of Egypt?"

Gideon may have thought that the age of miracles was past, but he was standing on the brink of another age of miracles, one that he would experience firsthand. We seem to be in a generation similar to Gideon's. In times of world unrest, God always sends a message to highlight the significance and urgency of the impending crisis.

ABOVE HIS WORD?

The Bible describes many times when God has used men and women as His messengers. As we shall see, they appear whenever God needs a special message for a special time.

Let's look at the ministry of Ellen White. Was she a prophetess of God?

One small accusation is that Ellen White could not be a prophet because the Bible says, "Let your women keep silent in the churches" (1 Corinthians 14:34). However, we know from the Bible that God does speak through female prophets. Miriam, Deborah, Anna and Isaiah's wife were all prophets in the Old Testament. In the New Testament, Phillip's daughters are called prophets. It also says in Acts 2 that the "sons and daughters" will receive the spirit of prophecy. The Bible makes it very clear that the gift of prophecy is not restricted to men.

A more urgent and potentially disastrous misunderstanding is that the teachings of Ellen While in the Seventh-day Adventist church are placed on a higher plane than the Bible. Of course, we know that every church has members with "cultic" beliefs, and the Seventh-day Adventist church is no exception. Some followers look to other individuals to dictate all they are supposed to do, and it may be that some Adventists have taken their adoration of Ellen White to cultic levels.

For the record, I have been teaching the Adventist message for years, and I have never attempted to prove the Sabbath or any other Adventist teaching through the writings of Ellen White. The Bible is powerful enough to stand on its own, which is why Ellen White clung to its truths so fiercely.

However, we know that most denominations have a founder or leader whom they obviously greatly admire. John Wesley was a Spirit-filled individual inspired by God. And led by God, the Methodist church grew under his leadership. Martin Luther is another man I greatly admire. Was he inspired? I believe he was. In every great movement, God uses men and women as spiritual leaders.

Indeed, I have never heard of the Lord using an angel to start a religious movement. He relies on people to do that work. Unfortunately, people often get stuck on the messenger, and not the message. Some elevate John Wesley to unnecessarily worshipful heights, while others say that "If Luther didn't say it, I don't believe it." Some Adventists may do the same thing with Ellen White, forgetting that prophets are people too. Not every aspect of a prophet's life or everything she may have said should be taken as divine inspiration.

UNDERSTANDING THE PROPHETS BETTER

The Bible gives us many examples that show how prophets made human errors in their day-to-day lives. Miriam, Moses' sister, is a good example. Though she was a prophet, she was also somewhat of a bigot (Exodus 15:20). As the story goes in Numbers 12, God smote Miriam with leprosy for speaking against Moses' Ethiopian wife! This failing did not mean that she wasn't a prophet. It simply means that when they are not doing the will of God, a prophet's or prophetess' mouth may at times get them into a heap of trouble.

Nathan was also an Old Testament prophet. In 1 Chronicles 17, we're told how David wished to build a temple for the Lord that would be at least as beautiful as his home—because, while He lived in a palace, the ark of God was still housed in a temporary tent. Gradually,

David gathered the resources to build a magnificent temple. 1 Chronicles 17:1, 2 says, "Now it came to pass, when David was dwelling in his house, that David said to Nathan the prophet, 'See now, I dwell in an house of cedar but the ark of the covenant of the Lord is under tent curtains.' Then Nathan said to David, 'Do all that is in your heart; for God is with you.'"

Nathan and David were friends. I can almost hear Nathan say: "Go for it, David, God is with you." Was that a prophetic message? No, because later that night, Nathan received a message from God: "But it happened that night, that the word of God came to Nathan, saying: 'Go and tell My servant David, "Thus says the Lord: 'You shall not build Me a house to dwell in'"" (1 Chronicles 17:3, 4). Nathan, a prophct, had spoken too soon, offering up his own judgment! Nathan was a prophet, but he was also a fallible human being.

Samuel was also a prophet, perhaps one of the greatest. But was his every thought a divine revelation? In 1 Samuel 16:6, we find him searching for an adequate king for Israel. "And so it was, when [the sons of Jesse] came, that he looked at Eliab, and said, 'Surely the Lord's anointed is before Him.'"

Samuel is thinking, "This one has to be the one. Look at him—he's handsome, tall, and gracious." Instead, the Bible says: "But the Lord said to Samuel, 'Do not look at his appearance or at the height of his stature, because I have refused him. For the Lord does not see as man sees; for man looks at the outward appearance, but the Lord looks at the heart'" (1 Samuel 16:7).

Are you beginning to see a pattern here? Prophets were people like you and me who had personal opinions. When the Lord spoke to them directly or through an angel, this was the Word of God. When they were out shopping in the markets bargaining for the best price, this was not the result of revelation!

Likewise, some people have felt that when Ellen White said, "Please pass the salt," they were to write it down and contemplate the prophetic significance of her statement. Yet as we have discovered, that is simply not biblical.

In the New Testament, Paul illustrated the humanness of prophets. Was Paul a prophet? I think that most of us would agree that Paul was a prophet in every sense. But in 1 Corinthians 7:6, he is very careful to differentiate his own opinion from the Word of the Lord. What did he mean when he said: "But I say this as a concession, not as a commandment." Essentially, he meant that his opinion regarding marriage at that time was *his* judgment, not divine revelation. He illustrated this again in 1 Corinthians 7:25, when he says, "Now concerning virgins: I have no commandment from the Lord: yet I give judgment as one whom the Lord in His mercy has made trustworthy." We see another illustration of this in 2 Corinthians 11:17, when Paul says: "What I speak, I speak not according to the Lord, but as it were foolishly, in this confidence of boasting." In other words, he's saying, "Now, it's not the Lord that is telling me to say this because I am going to boast like a fool." As you can see, all through the Bible we find a pattern of prophets behaving like everyday people.

Seventh-day Adventists teach that Ellen White had a special relationship with God—she was a prophet who said many amazing things. But she was also human, and the church as an organization has never forgotten this distinction. The principle remains as true today as it was in Bible times: the message is greater than the messenger. The content is greater than the container.

HUMAN COUNSEL VS. DIVINE UTTERANCE

A very close friend of mine knew Ellen White. My friend's father was also one of Mrs. White's contemporaries. He was very successful and extremely creative in his methods of holding the attention of his audiences. At one evangelistic meeting, he created papier-mâché beasts to depict the visions of Daniel and Revelation. The stage was designed so that at the right moment, an assistant would pull open a trap door with the help of ropes and pulleys. The paper beasts rose up onto the stage, creating a fascinating visual display.

This event caused a flurry of correspondence to Ellen White. Many regarded the tactic as a terrible form of sensationalism. Ellen White responded: "He is working for God. We need to think of creative means to keep the attention of the people and to help them visualize the messages." In other words, "Leave him alone. I think what he is doing is great." This was her judgment of the situation at hand—it was her opinion based on a lot of personal experience but not a specific revelation from God.

Similarly, the judgment she has exercised in simple human affairs has often been ripped from the context of the moment. She once offered my friend's mother her sympathy when her husband became ill. She counseled, "Do all that you can for him because the Lord has a great work for him to do." Of course, his wife did all she could do to care for him, but despite her efforts, he died. The widow was inconsolable because she felt that she must not have done all that she could to aid her husband's recovery, for the Lord had spoken and said that he still had a great work remaining.

However, Ellen White wrote another letter that explained, "I was just speaking like anyone else would talk, saying he's doing a great work. I was sharing my sympathy and saying, do what you can for him. I was endorsing his work. It was not a divine utterance. You did everything that you could and the Lord saw fit that he pass away."

In other words, we should recognize the distinction between the common and the sacred. Certainly Ellen White did. Her grocery list should be treated differently than her inspired writings, such as *Steps to Christ.*

THE PLAGIARISM CHARGE

Some call Ellen White a plagiarist. You can read a book called *The White Lie,* written by a former Seventh-day Adventist minister who accuses Ellen White of literary theft. He was once an avid supporter of Ellen White until he read words that seemed too much like something Mrs. White wrote—so close that he thought, "She copied this!" Obviously, this shattered his confidence because he deeply respected her—and suddenly it seemed she had taken divine credit for something she did not write.

Plagiarism is a complicated accusation. Technically, it's stealing creative material and profiting from it without giving the original author credit. Another term, called literary borrowing, also happens quite frequently. As you are probably aware, Bible writers borrowed frequently from other writers without giving credit to them. The gospels mirror each other greatly—as much as 90 percent of the Gospel of Matthew parallels the Gospel of Mark. However, Matthew has never been called a plagiarist.

By the close of her seventy-year ministry, her literary productions totaled approximately 100,000 pages, including letters, diaries, periodical articles, pamphlets, and books. Yet of all the material she wrote, only a handful of writings appear to contain wording that is similar to the works of others. (Interestingly, John Bunyan, the writer of *Pilgrim's Progress,* was also accused of plagiarism. So was John Wesley, for that matter.)

We live in a time when everybody wants credit where credit is due. Copyrights and royalties have been implemented to safeguard and benefit the originator. Yet in the 1800s, the vestiges of the spiritual revolution lingered on, and these included the belief that inspired information belonged to everybody. To say, "Yes, you can use my material but be sure to give me the credit," would have been a foreign idea to them. God's wisdom was for all people, and no human could take credit for it. Thus it was common practice in Ellen White's day for many writers to employ concepts from others without giving the kind of credit sought by today's critics. They believed that biblical truths and principles were public domain.

Solomon wrote: "Is there anything new under the sun?" Very few people have purely original thoughts. Mark Twain commented that every writer is a plagiarist because nobody has new ideas anymore. I preach week after week—do you think that everything I have to say is original? In preparation for sermons, I gather information wherever I can all week long. I don't often give specific credit to others for my ideas. Sometimes I read the *Reader's Digest* on the plane and forget what I have read, until a year later some phrase in an article resurfaces in my mind. I might even incorporate it into a sermon or article without ever giving citation.

In 1980, Vincent L. Ramick, a Catholic attorney (with Dillar, Ramick, & Wright, Ltd.) in Washington, D.C., investigated the plagiarism accusation against Ellen White. He found no legal grounds for such emotionally charged allegations. Indeed, no legal claim was ever filed against Mrs. White or her estate. While researching her work, Mr. Ramick spent more than 300 hours reviewing Ellen White's material. He said that of all her books, *The Great Controversy* was his favorite. When asked what he thought of Ellen White's writings, he said, "The shocking thing was that Mrs. White moved me. In all candor she moved me. I am a Roman Catholic, but Catholic, Protestant, whatever, she moved me and I think her writings should move anybody unless he is permanently biased."

A FALSE PROPHET?

Many, of course, simply argue that Ellen White was a false prophet. Admittedly, I often wonder if people making such a drastic claim have ever read her writings. At other times, I realize that her writings are of such a high caliber that when she calls for people to turn away from sin and seek righteousness, many simply become uncomfortable. Charging that "it sounds like it is all about righteousness by works," they then condemn her work as heresy. Sometimes it seems that in order to feel comfortable, they must not only avoid her message, they must slander her.

Yet Ellen White considered her own lifestyle and Christian practice to be accountable, such that even leaders from other churches said, "We would never question her sincerity and Christian commitment. She is a godly woman." She spent much of her time feeding and helping others while she traveled to the far corners of the earth. While other so-called prophets were living in palatial homes hoarding book royalties, Ellen White lived modestly near Elmshaven, California, where she committed the money from her books to Christian ministry. She spent 70 of her 87 years in the work of ministry; from the time she was 17 years old, she had nearly 2,000 dreams and visions. Even radio legend Paul Harvey, in one of his broadcasts, endorsed some of her visions as the "Incredible Prophecies of Ellen White."

People often wonder how Ellen White could ever be considered a prophet of God. Many have questioned her lack of formal education, wondering how she could boldly tackle topics such as health, medicine, agriculture, and education. How could she be so knowledgeable about these topics when she left school in the third grade? And how could such a frail woman be the leader of a great world movement?

We should be careful with these lines of questioning. God does not always use people who have impressive titles. In fact, more often than not, it seems that God uses simple people, such as fishermen and shepherds, to perform great works for Him.

As such, formal education is not always a criterion for greatness in God's estimate. In Acts 4:13, Peter and John made their defense before the Sanhedrin, the intellectuals of Israel. "Now when they saw the boldness of Peter and John, and perceived that they were uneducated and untrained men (meaning that they were unlettered and did not hold degrees) … they marveled. And they realized that they had been with Jesus."

So far as we know, Jesus was also unlettered but brilliant. When he was 12 years old, he confounded the wise men in the temple.

I'd like to return for a moment to the charge that Ellen White is a false prophet because some hold her works in higher esteem than the Bible. This is a charge I don't mind addressing because it is one of the things that turned me away from the Latter-day Saints. Every time I found something in the Bible that conflicted with Mormon teachings, a member would use Joseph Smith's writings to back the teachings up. They explained that the teachings of Smith are "new light," and new light supersedes the "old light" of the Bible.

Those baptized into the Seventh-day Adventist church today take a vow that the Bible is the only rule of faith and practice for the Christian. Ellen White's name appears nowhere in that statement. Her own words record this simple fact:

> "I recommend to you, dear reader, the Word of God as the rule of your faith and practice. By the Word we are to be judged. God has in the Word promised

to give visions in the last days, not for a new rule of faith, but for the comfort of His people and to correct those who err from the Bible truth."

—*Early Writings*, p. 78.

In these few sentences, she readily admits that the Word makes a provision that God will still speak, but it is not to preclude or assume prominence over the Bible. She added:

"Little heed is given to the Bible and the Lord has given lesser light [referring to her writings]. We are to regard the Bible as God's disclosure to us of eternal things, things of most consequence for us to know. By the world it is thrown aside as if the perusal of it were finished, but a thousand years of research would not exhaust the hidden treasures the Bible contains. Eternity alone will disclose the wisdom of this book, for it is the wisdom of an infinite mind. Shall we then cultivate a deep hunger for the productions of human authors and disregard the Word of God?"

—*Review and Herald*, January 20, 1903.

People who believe that Seventh-day Adventists hold human authors above the writings of the Bible are very much mistaken. As I mentioned earlier, there are misguided folk in every religious persuasion. Adventism is no exception. Some may carry Mrs. White's books to church but rarely their Bible—Ellen White would have rejected that kind of misplaced devotion.

Another accusation against Ellen White is that some of her prophecies have not come true. Many of these stem from confusion about what her prophecies meant, some of them from the fact that the fulfillment of those prophecies still lay in the future.

Of the many visions that Ellen White experienced, a small number were conditional. She once said that if people had a solid relationship with the Lord and accomplished the works that they were called to do, they might hasten the return of Jesus. When the Lord did not come, detractors said, "She must be a false prophet!" She responded to these claims by saying, "No, these were conditional on our doing certain things."

Are conditional prophecies simply a bait-and-switch tactic to deflect criticism against Adventism? In the Book of Jonah, we have a biblical example of a conditional prophecy. God tells Jonah in no uncertain terms that the city of Nineveh would be destroyed in 40 days if the people did not turn from their wicked ways. Fortunately, the Bible says that the city repented and God chose to spare the people. God also told Moses to lead the Jews into the Promised Land, having every intention of delivering this first generation to the land of milk and honey. But it was a promise that the children of Israel refused to believe. As a result, God allowed them to die in the wilderness and take their descendants into the land instead. There are other examples in which God's prophets made conditional prophecies.

THE INJURED PROPHET

As a child, Ellen Harmon was active, cheerful, and buoyant. One afternoon, as she was returning home from school, she was hit by a large stone, unintentionally thrown in her direction by a classmate. She was struck in the face and suffered a broken nose and probably a concussion. Three weeks of unconsciousness followed. The experience left her ill and debilitated.

Physicians gave her little hope of recovery as she floundered through her classes. At the age of 12, she made her last attempt at school, but again suffered failing health. However, her frugal and wise parents did not allow her to grow up in useless ignorance. From her mother she received a thorough, practical training and, as she was able, assisted her father in hat making.

In some ways, I can relate to Ellen White. I do not have a formal education, but I learned how to read. I used to tell my children, "Learn to read, and learn to do it well, because then you will be able to educate yourself." Ellen White did just that. She learned how to read, and she learned to do it well. Blessed with an insatiable desire to learn, she became a prolific reader, which may be one of the reasons she was charged with plagiarism.

Ellen White's early injury is often used to discount her visions. However, it is not typical for a broken nose to be a cause of brain damage. Indeed, if the visions that have inspired millions of people were caused by an errant stone, then I beg you to stone me.

Dr. Kellogg, a close friend of the family who did not mind disagreeing with Ellen White, believed Ellen White was inspired. He understood her visions as having come from God. He knew her closely, lived in her home and understood her physical state. As a trained physician, he never said the visions occurred as a result of a nervous condition.

AN ERRANT BELIEF

Another accusation that has been leveled against Ellen White, is that she believed in the "shut door theory." Most today have never even heard of this, but in 1844, when many in the Christian community thought that Jesus was going to come, there were no Seventh-day Adventists.

When Ellen White had her first vision at age the age of 17, she was among the group of Advent believers that was made up of Methodists, Baptists, and a few other denominations that kept the Sabbath on Sunday. They believed that those who had not accepted the message that Christ would return in 1844 could not be converted after the "door was shut" on

October 22, 1844—an allusion to the Bridegroom parable in Matthew 25.

Ellen White admitted that she once believed this misunderstanding. But after her first vision in December, 1844, she saw this belief to be wrong—much more work was yet to be done before Jesus would return. In responding to this charge in 1874, she wrote:

> "With my brethren and sisters, after the time had passed in forty-four I did believe no more sinners would be converted. But I never had a vision that no more sinners would be converted. And I am clear and free to state that no one has ever heard me say or ever read from my pen, statements which justify them in the charges they have made against me upon this point."[1]

However, it took approximately seven years before most of the other early Adventist leaders became settled in their conviction that Ellen was right—the door had not been shut against the world in 1844!

Is there a parallel that can be drawn from Scripture? Yes! After Jesus rose from the dead, and after the disciples were endorsed by the Holy Spirit on Pentecost, they *still* believed that only the Jews would be saved. On the day of Pentecost, when 3,000 people were baptized, they were all Jews. Later, 5,000 more people were baptized and who were they? Jews.

But several years after the crucifixion of Christ, Peter had a vision regarding the salvation of the Gentiles (Acts 10, 11). And after Paul's conversion, the gospel was gradually taken to the Gentiles. Slowly the apostles began to realize that salvation is not the exclusive domain of some special group of people. Did the apostles preach for Jesus before His death? Did they have misconceptions about the nature of Christ's ministry, even while they were out preaching for

Jesus? Absolutely! Up to the moment when Jesus was nailed to the cross, the disciples believed that He was going to establish an earthly kingdom. Yet despite their ignorance relating to His plan, they were preaching, healing, casting out devils, and raising the dead. They were Spirit-filled prophets working for Jesus even before they had all of their theology straightened out.

THE FRUIT OF A PROPHET

If God has a prophet who stirs people enough to create a great Christian movement, would it not stand to reason that he or she would also be the object of the devil's rage? Satan would be all too happy to paint God's messenger in a very unfavorable light. He attacks anyone and anything that glorifies the Lord, something that Jesus promised would happen. Jesus once said, "If they have done it to me, they will do it unto you." (See John 15:20).

Of course, anyone can make the claim that they are being persecuted by the devil. But Ellen White has something most do not have.

Jesus said of prophets, "You shall know them by their fruits" (see Matthew 7:16–20). Some say that the fruit of Ellen White's writing is a recipe for making a legalistic Christian. However, I want to share a professional survey that enabled researchers to study the differences in Christian attitudes and behaviors between those who read and believed the writings of Ellen White and those who did not. The results were very revealing:

Eighty-five percent of those who frequently read and believed Ellen White's writings indicated that they had an intimate relationship with Jesus, as compared to the 59 percent of those who did not read her writings. Eighty-two percent of the readers had the assurance that they were right with God, while 59 percent of non-readers did not.

Daily personal Bible study was the habit of 82 percent of readers, while only 47 percent of non-readers acknowledged personal study.

Overall, those who studied the Bible in conjunction with Ellen White's writings felt better prepared for Christian witnessing, felt more at home with their fellow church members, prayed more, gave more support toward local soul winning, and were generally more willing to help their neighbors. In short, their Christian experience was stronger, more active, and more positive.[2]

Ellen White's writings inspire change in hearts that are seeking truth. When her books are sincerely read, they will not create legalists—they will test the soul. They will provide powerful insights on the life of Christ and His amazing plan for our salvation. At the end of her life, with her last breath, Ellen White whispered, "I know in whom I have believed." Far from being a legalist, she only believed in the high standard that the Bible has set before all of us.

Endnotes

[1] Herbert E. Douglass, *Messenger of the Lord* (Nampa, ID: Pacific Press Publishing Association, 1998), p. 562.

[2] *Ministry,* October, 1982.

Chapter Four

A DVENTISTS AND THE HEALTH MESSAGE

S eventh-day Adventists are considered especially odd by other religious faiths because we still believe in the health laws prescribed in the Bible's Old Testament.

Of course, most denominations believe in the basic health laws of the Bible, to some degree. The law of cleanliness seems like common sense to most of us. However, when the Bible begins stipulating the specifics of what to eat and what not to eat, accusations of legalism once again surface.

In this chapter, I hope to clarify the common misunderstandings related to the Adventist health message that cause many to stumble over our teachings. It is my desire to explain in biblical terms why Adventists continue to practice and share the message that God really does care about how we treat the bodies He created.

The Bible shows us that Jesus is very interested in physical health. He understood that it is difficult to be a joyful Christian when we're feeling sick. Matthew 4:23 records: "And Jesus went about all Galilee teaching in their synagogues, preaching the gospel of the kingdom, and healing all kinds of sickness and all kinds of disease among the people."

God wants us to live life to the fullest and to prosper physically: "Beloved, I pray that you may prosper in all things and be in health, just as your soul prospers" (3 John 2). All the sickness and disease in the world today is a result of sin, one way or another. Sickness eats away into our happiness and our ability to be useful to others. So when Christ healed the sick, He did so that they might serve God more efficiently and become better witnesses for Him.

Because Adventists accept this biblical principle, they have chosen to abstain from many substances which attack the body and defuse its defenses. One of these, alcoholic beverages, is particularly rejected in the Seventh-day Adventist church. Common sense tells us that it is difficult to grasp, accept, and follow the gospel while you're drunk—or even slightly "buzzed." All things are possible with God's help, of course, but as a general rule it is very difficult to share God's message with somebody who is drunk. I've had some drunks knock on my door telling me they want to give their hearts to the Lord. They cry and accept Jesus, but then walk away and forget the entire experience once they are sober.

The clearer our minds, the more prepared we will be to understand the requirements of the gospel and appreciate our Lord's ultimate sacrifice for our sins. I think that you would also agree that it is much easier to resist other forms of temptation when your head is clear.

Of course, you don't necessarily have to drink Jack Daniels to have a foggy brain. Your mind can get foggy from eating a banana split. "Do not be deceived. God is not mocked; for whatever a man sows, that he will also reap" (Galatians 6:7). If you sow bushels of cholesterol, you will likely reap a heart attack as well as many other life-threatening diseases.

I don't want to get too deep into the nuts and bolts of dietary health in these few pages. But I do want to establish that God wants us to be healthy, and that He has given us some definite guidelines regarding what we should, and should not, eat.

Science and common sense overwhelmingly indicate that there is a relationship between what we eat and our health. To say that we can eat whatever we want and it will not hurt us is an insult to God. As a parent, you are concerned about the specifics of what your children eat. Do you read the labels and inspect for nutritional values? So if you care for your child that much, how much more does God care about you?

MEAT: THE CLEAN AND THE UNCLEAN

It's clear from Genesis that God did not create man to eat animals. His original plan for us was a vegetarian diet, and I believe there is strong evidence in the Bible that in the kingdom of heaven we will become vegetarians again. There will be no McDonald's or Burger Kings in heaven.

Science has proven that vegetarians have fewer incidences of heart disease, cancer, and diabetes than those who eat any kind of flesh. Incidentally, on average, Seventh-day Adventists live up to seven years longer than the rest of society.

Killing and eating animals came about as one of the consequences of sin. I've met hunters who ask, "If God didn't want us to eat meat, why did he make animals?" That certainly is primitive thinking!

Others say, "You can't be healthy unless you eat animals. We were intended to eat meat because God created us with canine teeth." But this just isn't true! Strikingly, some of the largest mammals on earth are vegetarian. For instance, a vegetarian diet can easily sustain an elephant. Gorillas have some of the biggest canine teeth of any primate, yet they are vegetarian. Everything about our digestive system works more efficiently when we follow God's original design. However, just as God made provision for divorce because of the hardness of people's hearts, He also made provision for us to eat some animals if we so choose.

God has made it clear that if we are going to eat animals, they need to meet certain qualifications. In short, they must be "clean." We can go as far back as Noah to see that God made a distinction in animal meat—that is, between the clean and unclean. Noah took clean animals into the ark by sevens and the unclean animals by twos. The Bible defines clean and unclean by saying: "You may eat any land animal that has divided hoofs and that also chews the cud" (Leviticus 11:2, 3, GNB). In other words, the animals that are technically safe to eat would be the deer, sheep, cow, and goat. A horse does not have a cloven foot, thus it is not clean. Likewise, the pig is a scavenger that is riddled with parasites.

In Leviticus 11, the Bible also addresses seafood. It states that those fish that are clean have scales and fins. Catfish and other bottom feeders are unclean. As a perfectly balanced ecosystem, God created some creatures to keep the environment clean. Thus, those animals that scavenge are not clean meats.

Among the birds, God simply stipulates that the foraging birds of the forest are clean. These include the turkey, quail, chicken, and dove. The carnivorous birds, such as the hawk and the vulture, are considered unclean.

These are undisputed Bible facts—the basic rules that separate the clean from the unclean.

MAKING THE UNCLEAN CLEAN?

Some Christians have insisted to me that because they are more spiritual than some, they can eat anything they want and it won't hurt them. I don't think any physician, Christian or not, would endorse that view!

Moreover, they also point to at least five New Testament passages that they believe negate the health concepts addressed in the Old Testament; yet all five are either misapplied or misquoted. I'd like to begin with Acts 10, in which Peter has an unusual vision.

Some say these verses give us freedom to eat anything we want. But this is nonsense! We know that this vision came to Peter at a time when the disciples were preaching exclusively to the Jews. Even as the Spirit of God was poured over them, the larger view of God's plan was given to them in small increments so they could more readily embrace it. At first, even the disciples did not conceive that there is no distinction between Jew and Gentile in God's eyes and that they should be preaching to everyone.

And so the story goes that Cornelius, a Roman Centurion, who prays to God and gives alms to the poor, receives a vision in which an angel tells him: "Your prayers and your alms have come up for a memorial before God. Now send men to Joppa, and send for Simon, whose surname is Peter. He is lodging with Simon, a tanner, whose house is by the sea. He will tell you what you must do" (Acts 10:4–6). Cornelius obeyed this command and sent his most trusted men to Joppa in search of Peter.

Meanwhile, Peter was on the roof praying before lunch when he received his vision from God. Acts 10:10–14 records: "He became very hungry and wanted to eat; but while they made ready, he fell into a trance and saw heaven opened, and an object like a great sheet bound at the four corners descending to him and let down to the earth. In it were all kinds of four-footed animals of the earth, wild beasts, creeping things, and birds of the air. And a voice came to him, 'Rise, Peter; kill, and eat.' But Peter said, 'Not so, Lord! For I have never eaten any thing common or unclean.' And a voice spoke to him again the second time, 'What God has cleansed you must not call common.'"

This is where people get turned around. I've been asked, "Doug, God cleansed everything on the sheet. All animals are clean now, right?" It is significant that this sheet is lowered from the heavens three times, with Peter continuing to answer, "Not so, Lord." In verse 17, Peter begins to wonder what the Lord is trying to tell him.

A little later, we can easily see that God was simply talking to Peter about new truths, using Bible truths that he readily understood. In other words, the time had come for Peter to preach the gospel to the Gentiles. As Peter wondered about the significance of this strange vision, three Gentile men approached the house and said, "Come and preach to us." God's immaculate timing explains to us the meaning of Peter's vision clearly.

But just to ensure that no one would take this vision as the go-ahead to eat unclean animals, Peter gives the vision's interpretation. At Cornelius' house, he said: "You know how unlawful it is for a Jewish man to keep company with or go to one of another nation. But God has shown me that I should not call any man common or unclean" (Verse 28). The vision wasn't about pigs, but about people!

God gave this message to Peter in the form of an allegory. He did not mean that all animals were clean and could be safely eaten. Remember, Peter does not eat anything from the sheet! And this is one of the best arguments in favor of God's health laws. This vision occurred several years after Jesus died, and Peter still refused to eat common or unclean meat.

The ending of this story is especially powerful. Listen! "Then Peter opened his mouth, and said: 'In truth I perceive that God shows no partiality. But in every nation whoever fears Him and works righteousness is accepted by Him'" (Acts 10:34, 35).

SEEKING OUR OWN

Another Bible passage that is frequently used to do away with God's health laws is 1 Corinthians 10:24–28. Much of the discussion in the New Testament revolved around Jews accepting Christianity. One of the struggles for these Jews was accepting the new, non-Jewish Christians who had been accustomed to eating everything. Not only did they eat pigs and everything else, they also offered food in honor of their pagan gods.

Paul explained in 1 Corinthians 10:24, 25: "No one should be looking to his own interests, but to the interests of others. You are free to eat anything sold in the meat-market, without asking any questions because of your conscience."

But Paul is not telling these church members to go to the meat market and buy whatever carcass pleases them—with no thought as to whether it is a dog, horse, or pig.

Instead, Paul is saying: "You don't need to ask whether or not this meat was offered to idols because once you know, it doesn't change the meat, but it changes your influence." If you know that it was offered to idols and then ate it anyway, it could be a stumbling block to other Christians.

Paul adds: "If an unbeliever invites you to a meal and you decide to go, eat what is set before you, without asking any questions because of your conscience" (10:27, GNB). Some Christians pounce on this statement, saying, "Doug, eat whatever is set before you. It might be a pig with an apple in its mouth, but just eat it." But Paul is still talking about food offered to idols, a common practice in Corinth. If a Christian is invited to an unbeliever's home, he should not embarrass his host by making inquiries as to the whether the meal on the table had first been sacrificed to the false gods of his host. Paul is not sanctioning food that the Christian knows is forbidden by God. His argument here is regarding food offered to idols and does not address the fitness of food for a healthy diet.

OUR HOLY TEMPLE

Our body is the temple of the Holy Spirit (1 Corinthians 3:16, 17; 6:19, 20). For you to bring an unclean animal as an "offering" and have it consumed upon the altar of your digestive system is a great insult to God. The prophet Daniel was willing to die rather than defile himself with the unclean Babylonian food. And the result was that, not only was Daniel honored with a long life, he was also honored with wisdom ten times above all the other wise men (Daniel 1).

With this in mind, let's turn to Romans 14:1, 2, which says: "Receive one who is weak in the faith, but not to disputes over doubtful things. For one believes he may eat all things, but he who is weak eats only vegetables." Believe it or not, I have been told that I am weak because I am vegetarian. Of course, we have already discussed that some of the biggest and strongest animals in the world are elephants and gorillas. That notion is simply ridiculous and easily rejected by modern nutritional principles.

But is Paul really saying that all who eat vegetables are physically weak? Not at all. Rather, he is saying: "He that is weak in faith doesn't eat the animals that are sacrificed to idols because he thinks that he would be breaking a rule, thus stumbling over issues of righteousness by works, especially rules that are not really binding on him."

Still, are you aware that the apostles disagreed on this issue? In Acts 15:20, where the apostles are trying to decide what priorities the Gentiles should follow, it says: "Write to them to abstain from things polluted by idols, from sexual immorality, from things strangled, and from blood." In other words, don't eat foods that have been sacrificed to idols. Yet Paul said that if it doesn't bother you, don't ask any questions. For him it is not an issue because an idol is nothing to a child of God.

But there is more in this New Testament counsel to Christians. These days, meat is not generally prepared according to the Jewish law or in accordance with this apostolic consensus. Today's meat is full of blood, whether prepared in a restaurant or at home. You rarely hear Christians talking about this verse because it is clearly a message to New Testament Gentile Christians—it is part of the health message that is largely ignored by Christians. I find it troubling that they use these verses to support their beliefs, while ignoring those parts that contradict them.

RECEIVING MEATS WITH THANKSGIVING?

Some of the most controversial of these troubling verses are contained in 1 Timothy 4:1–5. Like the others, it is misapplied by meat-eaters who want Paul's words to mean something that they do not. It says, "Now the Spirit speaketh expressly, that in the latter times some shall depart from the faith, giving heed to seducing spirits, and doctrines of devils; Speaking lies in hypocrisy; having their conscience seared with a hot iron; Forbidding to marry, and commanding to abstain from meats [food], which God hath created to be received with thanksgiving of them which believe and know the truth" (KJV).

Clearly, this is describing a church that would forbid some of its people to marry and also forbid the eating of certain things that God gave us to eat, at certain times. Some Christians seize upon this part: "For every creature of God is good, and nothing to be refused, if it be received with thanksgiving." These same Christians tell me, "See, every creature of God is good." But are these people also talking about squid, snails, frogs, turtles and ants?

People eat some bizarre things. But when they say the Bible teaches that all creatures are good, that's an extreme statement with extreme consequences. What about cannibalism? When we look carefully at what Paul is saying, he is specifically limiting his remarks to those foods that God has created for eating. He is not elaborating on the distinctions between clean and unclean foods. Further, he is saying that church regulations that forbid the eating of certain foods for religious purposes are totally without biblical foundation. Many of us accept arguments for ourselves that we would never accept from our children. Suppose your children prepare for breakfast by setting out the box of Sugar Frosted Flakes and the sugar bowl. They begin by filling the bowl with Sugar Frosted Flakes and then proceed to dump several spoonfuls of sugar over the top. You would say, "Hey, wait a minute. That's enough!" What if your child responded, "It doesn't matter what I eat, Mom. It's about to be sanctified by prayer." Would you parents accept that?

I would like to know what makes us think that we can eat all kinds of contemptible things that both science and the Bible tell us are an abomination. The Bible says, "Do not be deceived. God is not mocked." We are mocking God by eating unclean, filthy animals and saying, "All I have to do is pray over it." These verses in Timothy clearly specify that what is being referred to are foods already sanctified by God. It does not say anything about declaring certain foods clean or unclean.

UNWASHED HANDS

Another appropriate text to address is Mark 7:1–7, which says: "Then the Pharisees and some of the scribes came together to Him, having come from Jerusalem. Now when they saw some of His disciples eat bread with defiled, that is, with unwashed hands, they found fault." What is the issue here? Is this verse speaking of what to eat or what kind of hands the food was to be eaten with?

It's important to see that no type of food is ever mentioned in this passage. The issue is whether the disciples had ceremonially washed their hands or not. "For the Pharisees, and all the Jews do not eat unless they wash their hands in a special way, holding the tradition of the elders." Obviously, this story focuses on tradition, not on a Bible commandment regarding food or anything else. The passage continues: "When they come from the marketplace, they do not eat unless they wash." The disciples ignored these ceremonial washings, arousing the reproach of the Pharisees. "Then the

Pharisees and scribes asked Him, 'Why do Your disciples not walk according to the tradition of the elders, but eat bread with unwashed hands?' He answered and said to them, 'Well did Isaiah prophesy of you hypocrites, as it is written: "This people honors Me with their lips, But their heart is far from Me. And in vain they worship Me, Teaching as doctrines the commandments of men."'"

Notice also in this verse that Jesus is addressing the "commandments of men." The verse does not address the issue of clean or unclean foods, because that was a doctrine given by God. Jesus is condemning their ceremonial washings, their legalism, which are commandments of men. Matthew 15:11, a parallel passage, says: "Not what goes into the mouth defiles a man; but what comes out of the mouth, this defiles a man." This is said in the same context as in Mark.

What does it mean? It was an exciting day when I first read this verse. I was in the process of becoming convicted to give up drugs and alcohol when I came across this Scripture. I thought, "Praise the Lord! I don't have to worry about what I put in my mouth!" I continued to smoke and drink and then it dawned on me—what goes into your mouth will affect what comes out.

But Christ was trying to emphasize that purity of heart is not based on whether you have eaten with ceremonially washed hands. He elaborated in Mark 7:18, 19: "Are you thus without understanding also? Do you not perceive that whatever enters a man from outside cannot defile him, because it does not enter his heart but his stomach, and is eliminated, thus purifying all foods?"

The context is not dealing with biological uncleanness, but with the ceremonial uncleanness supposedly derived from unwashed hands. In other words, the issue is not what is being eaten but how.

A Biblical Principle

When trying to grasp Bible truths, always remember that when God makes an explicit command to do something one way, He will make an equally explicit command should He choose to revoke it later. You won't have to dig around for ambiguous verses and put great effort into twisting them around to fit your understanding. When God says, "The seventh day is the Sabbath," you should not have to twist the New Testament upside down to try to make it say that it is not. He would tell us if the seventh-day Sabbath is no longer a binding commandment, or if it has been made into another day of the week. Of course, He has never made those changes.

Likewise, when God says, "Do not eat unclean animals, do not touch them. They are an abomination," He means just that. If God meant to change His mind, you would find permission in the New Testament to eat swine clearly spelled out. The silence about the Sabbath and unclean food in the New Testament is really quite stunning.

Our body is the temple of the Holy Spirit, and the Bible tells us that God expects us to take care of it. In 1 Corinthians 9:25, Paul wrote: "Everyone who competes for the prize is temperate in all things." Not only are Christians obligated to abstain from those things that God has forbidden, but we should also exercise temperance in those things that He freely gives.

When I think of biblical dietary commands, I like to think of the green, yellow, and red traffic signals. Of course, most of us know that green means go, yellow means exercise caution, and red means stop. We are told we have the green light on things like fruits, nuts, grains, and vegetables. And we have some bright red lights on things like tobacco, alcohol, and meats which God has declared unclean.

Meats declared clean are given the yellow light. Americans consume more meat than any other nation, and we also have many more times the amount of cancer. Countries in which people eat primarily beans and rice and an occasional piece of meat are far healthier.

Of course, Americans love to eat sweets—a "yellow light" food. We also face health issues such as obesity and diabetes. Sugar causes so many problems when used in excess that it certainly belongs in the yellow category, if not the red! The Bible says: "Do you not know that you are the temple of God and that the Spirit of God dwells in you?" (1 Corinthians 3:16). Paul also says in 1 Corinthians 6:19, 20: "Do you not know that your body is the temple of the Holy Spirit who is in you, whom you have from God, and you are not your own?"

Paul implores us to offer ourselves to God as a clean and acceptable sacrifice (Romans 12:1). We need clear minds more than ever in these last days to be better able to resist temptation.

We are the temple of God individually as well as collectively, and God wants to fill His temple with His Spirit. I challenge you to make your soul and your body available for His presence by accepting the health principles that He has so graciously given to us throughout the Bible.

Chapter Five

A DVENTISTS AND THE JUDGMENT

The subject of the sanctuary is unique to the Seventh-day Adventist church. It is probably the doctrine most widely ignored by contemporary churches, aside from the seventh-day Sabbath and the biblical health laws. Seventh-day Adventists have gleaned a special understanding about the plan of salvation from the powerful sanctuary picture. It is thus dear to the Adventist's heart.

Throughout the Bible, God has used many symbols to reach His people. Perhaps the most detailed of these are those wrapped up in the many layers of the sanctuary. When the children of Israel came out of Egypt, they first traveled south to Mount Sinai. Not only did they receive the Ten Commandments there, they also received instructions to build a traveling tabernacle, or sanctuary, in which God could "visibly" dwell among the Jews. It was a plan that would help the Israelites understand God better.

THE SANCTUARY OF MEANING

The sanctuary was comprised of three very specific parts: the courtyard, the holy place, and the most holy place. Only one entrance led into the courtyard, just as there is only one way to eternal life. Jesus said, "I am the door." Only one way in!

After proceeding through the door, the first steps led to the altar of burnt offering, just as the first step in becoming saved begins at Christ's sacrificial offering on the cross. A laver, a bronze basin for ceremonial washing, symbolized baptism—death from sin and rebirth. Thus the courtyard contained the symbols of the cross, of our acceptance of Jesus, and of baptism.

Three articles, the table of showbread, the candlestick with seven lamps, and the altar of incense, furnished the holy place. The Bible tells us that the lamp, kept alive with precious oil, is symbolic of the Holy Spirit. The table of bread represents the Word of God that nourishes us. The altar of incense is a symbol of prayer. The incense would waft over the curtain into the most holy place before the presence of God, just as our prayers go to Him.

A veil separated the holy place from the center of the entire sacrificial plan—a smaller room called the holy of holies. The Ark of the Covenant and the mercy seat were located in this area, symbolizing the dwelling place of God. Inside of the ark, the Ten Commandments were placed along with a small pot of manna and Aaron's rod that had budded. These symbolized God's authority and discipline, as well as His ability to provide for His people.

The earthly sanctuary continues to speak to us today. Because it was a reflection of the heavenly sanctuary (Exodus 25:8, 9) Adventists spend much time looking at the sanctuary service for meaning.

THE SANCTUARY PROPHECY

Daniel speaks of a prophecy relating to the power of the beast and the antichrist that would one day persecute God's people:

> "He even exalted himself as high as the Prince of the host; and by him the daily sacrifices were taken away, and the place of His sanctuary was cast down. Because of transgression, an army was given over to the horn to oppose the daily sacrifices; and he

cast truth down to the ground. He did all this and prospered. Then I heard a holy one speaking; and another holy one said to that certain one who was speaking, 'How long will the vision be, concerning the daily sacrifices and the transgression of desolation, the giving of both the sanctuary and the host to be trampled under foot?' And he said to me, 'For two thousand three hundred days; then the sanctuary shall be cleansed.'"

—Daniel 8:11–14.

Toward the end of this vision, Daniel fainted. It was too much for him to see God's people virtually annihilated, God blasphemed, the plan of salvation distorted, and the truth being cast to the ground. It was simply too overwhelming for him to watch.

In Daniel 9:25, an angel comes to the perplexed prophet to comfort him and give the starting point of this prophecy: "Know therefore and understand, That from the going forth of the command To restore and build Jerusalem until Messiah the Prince, There shall be seven weeks and sixty-two weeks." He adds that it would be three-and-a-half years after the start of the Messiah's ministry that God would cause the sacrifices to cease. We know the Messiah was anointed around A.D. 27, and that He died on the cross around A.D. 31. Like the prophecy says, God continued to confirm the covenant for another three-and-a-half years after Christ, the Sacrifice, was cut off. You may remember that Stephen was stoned after he made his final appeal to the Jewish leaders. After his death, persecution of Christians arose and the gospel was extended to the Gentiles. These first 490 years are clearly outlined in Acts 8.

But wait! Daniel's prophecy says "days" not "years"! So where did I come up with "days"? In Ezekiel we are told: "I have appointed thee a day for a year" (Ezekiel 4:6, KJV). Jesus also gave us an interesting example of a day representing a year. When adversaries of Christ said, "Herod is coming for you; he has already killed John!" Jesus said, "Go and tell him that I perform miracles and heal today and tomorrow, and the third day I will be perfected" (See Luke 13:31, 32). Did Jesus only preach three more days? John the Baptist was killed six months into Jesus' ministry, yet He preached three more years, not three days.

Now let's get back to Daniel, where it says that the sanctuary would be cleansed in 2,300 days. Using the day/year principle, if we add 2,300 to 457 B.C. (the date of the edict to rebuild Jerusalem), it brings us to A.D. 1844 (Remember that there is no zero year, so it goes directly from 1 B.C. to A.D. 1) The edict to rebuild Jerusalem is one of the most firmly accepted dates in the Bible! Ezra 7 gives the account of the final command to restore and build Jerusalem. Artaxerxes' decree supporting the new building project was given in the year 457 B.C., and thus begins the 2,300 days, after which "the sanctuary shall be cleansed."

THE GREAT DISAPPOINTMENT

Here is where it gets interesting. Many have said that the Seventh-day Adventist church grew out of a false interpretation regarding Jesus' Second Coming. This is both somewhat true and somewhat misleading. The Seventh-day Adventist church didn't exist in 1844—it didn't officially organize until 1863. However, a great spiritual revival, called the "Great Advent Movement," began in the early 1800s. Different people from many Christian denominations around the world began to study Daniel's prophecy. Many discovered that the 2300-year prophecy would end in the early 1840s.

Eventually they concluded that Jesus would return in the autumn of 1844—the time when the sanctuary would be cleansed. Although their math was correct, they came to the erroneous conclusion that the earth would be cleansed with fire in 1844. All around the world, Bible teachers were predicting the return of Christ with tremendous conviction. It caused a great revival.

It might be good to pause and clarify that the word "advent" means people who believe in the coming of Jesus. In a way, most Christians today are "Adventists"! In 1844, everyone from Baptists and Methodists, to people from many other denominations were feverishly anticipating the fast-approaching "coming of Jesus." They believed that Jesus would be returning in that year—and as we all know, they were wrong. The period following this error is called "The Great Disappointment." Out of this disappointment the foundation of the Seventh-day Adventist church was laid.

How would you live your life if you believed Christ would be returning next month? You and I would be spending a lot of time on our knees. And when we weren't praying, we would be out telling our friends and family members to make themselves right with God. This is exactly what Christians did during the "Great Advent Movement."

Of course, when Jesus did not come, the scoffers had a field day. It must have been a difficult time for deeply committed Christians. But a small group took courage from each other and determined to meet and study the Scriptures, in part to understand where they went wrong.

Among these early believers who believed that something important happened in 1844 were Ellen Harmon, a Methodist, Joseph Bates, who had roots in the Christian Church, and still others from Baptist backgrounds. Again and again, they looked at the date, and as far as they could tell, everything pointed to 1844.

SANCTUARY REDISCOVERED

Seventh-day Adventists have been accused of dreaming up the sanctuary doctrine as a cover-up for the embarrassment they endured in 1844. However, if you read the Bible from cover to cover, you will see that the sanctuary is mentioned everywhere. Where does Isaiah have his conversion experience? He was in vision in the sanctuary. The Book of Revelation also speaks very specifically about the temple in heaven.

That small group of studious Adventists in the 1840s soon discovered that the Bible never said that Jesus would cleanse the earth with fire in 1844. Most importantly, the Bible doesn't ever refer to the earth as a sanctuary. So what is the sanctuary?

Two sanctuaries are mentioned in the Old Testament in two very different localities—a sanctuary on earth, and one in heaven: "Then the temple of God was opened in heaven" (Revelation 11:19).

We know that the earthly sanctuary was constructed with human hands and built for the purpose of assisting humans in knowing God. Throughout the year, the priest would enter the holy place to offer sacrifices for the people, symbolizing that they were cleansed and forgiven. Obviously there was no virtue in the lamb's blood to cleanse from sin, but its blood was a symbol of Jesus, the Lamb of God, who takes away the sin of the world! (John 1:29). Thus the earthly sanctuary not only pointed to the coming of Jesus to this earth, but also to *why* He would come.

In Leviticus 16, we read about the ceremony that took place once a year during the Day of Atonement. Trumpets would be blown 10 days prior to that day, calling people to perform a self-evaluation—a time of prayer in which they would ask God to purge them from their sins. The high priest, bearing the sins of Israel, would then enter the holy of holies to make atonement for the people.

Do we have a High Priest today? Yes, and the book of Hebrews identifies Him as Jesus, who has been making intercession for us. He has borne our sins as well as carried our sorrows and He stands ready, night and day, to provide "grace to help in time of need" (Hebrews 4:16).

While on earth, Jesus did much of His preaching from the earthly sanctuary, the temple in Jerusalem. Remember when He cast many from the temple, saying, "Do not make My Father's house a house of merchandise" (John 2:16)? And when Christ walked away from of the temple, He said, "Behold your house is left unto you desolate. There will not be left one stone upon one another" (See Matthew 23:38-24:2). This meant that with the destruction of Jerusalem, the purpose of the earthly temple would be fulfilled.

WHAT IS THE EARTHLY SANCTUARY TODAY?

The people challenged Jesus' statement about the temple by asking, "What sign do You show to us, since You do these things?" (John 2:18). Jesus answered: "Destroy this temple, and in three days I will raise it up." Of course, the Jews were astounded! It took 46 years to build the temple, and Jesus was claiming He could raise it up in three days. But as John explains, Jesus was referring to His physical body.

The church is also called the body of Christ. We're told in 1 Peter 2:5: "You also as living stones, are being built up a spiritual house, a holy priesthood, to offer up spiritual sacrifices acceptable to God through Jesus Christ." In other words, you and I are the temple of God—we are the body of Christ. Ephesians 2:19–22 adds:

> "Now, therefore, you are no longer strangers and foreigners, but fellow citizens with the saints and members of the household of God, having been built on the foundation of the apostles and prophets, Jesus Christ Himself being the chief cornerstone, in whom the whole building, being joined together, grows into a holy temple in the Lord, in whom you also are being built together for a habitation of God in the Spirit."

When Jesus was on trial for His crucifixion, two witnesses could not be found who could agree about the charges. Finally, they found two who came close and they quoted something that Jesus once said. Mark 14:58 records their testimony: "We heard Him say, 'I will destroy this temple that is made with hands, and within three days I will build another made without hands.'" They did misquote Jesus slightly, because Jesus didn't say "I will destroy this temple made with hands," but only, "I will raise up another one made without hands." This reconstructed church "made without hands" was His church of committed Christians.

So how many temples are there presently? The answer is still two. There is one on earth and one in heaven. According to Scripture, God's people are His earthly temple.

THE SANCTUARY IN HEAVEN

Returning once more to Daniel 8 and the vision of 2,300 days, we know that the sanctuary was to be cleansed in 1844. But which sanctuary? The answer is both, and here is why: First, without the shedding of blood, priests have nothing to offer. Likewise, until Jesus shed His blood on the cross, He was not yet able to plead His blood in the heavenly temple—He had nothing to offer as a remission for our sins. When Christ rose from the grave and Mary reached out to worship Him, He said, "Do not cling to Me, for I have not yet ascended to My Father" (John 20:17).

When Christ ascended into heaven, He activated the final work of the heavenly sanctuary. And for 1,900 years, Jesus continued with His ministry as the priest of the daily offerings until 1844. Hebrews 6:18–20 says:

> "That by two immutable things, in which it was impossible for God to lie, we might have strong consolations, who have fled for refuge to lay hold of the hope set before us. This hope we have as an anchor

of the soul, both sure and steadfast, and which enters the Presence behind the veil, where the forerunner is for us entered, even Jesus, having become High Priest for ever according to the order of Melchizedek."

Why was there a veil separating the holy place from the holy of holies? Because the Shekinah glory, which streamed out from the Ark of the Covenant, was blinding, and in most circumstances, lethal. The sinful condition of the human heart cannot bear to be in the presence of God. Legend even has it that a blue cord was tied around the priest's leg before he entered the most holy place on the Day of Atonement. Should he collapse inside, they would need it to drag him out!

But Jesus in the heavenly sanctuary does not need a veil to separate Him from His Father. Once more, use your imagination for a minute: The earthly temple had wall coverings that were woven with angels, and golden angels hovered over the ark. Do you think that the heavenly temple needs wallpaper or that God needs "gold" angels in heaven! Do you think that the heavenly temple shares the same dimensions of 15 feet across or do you think that it could be five light years across? The earthly sanctuary is a microcosm to help us, who have limited spiritual vision, to see salvation truth.

Thus in 1844 Christ actually entered the final phase of His ministry as our High Priest, as is represented by the Most Holy Place in the earthly sanctuary. His work there continues to this day, but will soon come to an end.

THE JUDGMENT THAT BEGAN IN 1844

Revelation 14:6, 7 says:

"Then I saw another angel flying in the midst of heaven, having the everlasting gospel to preach to those who dwell on the earth; to every nation, tribe, tongue, and people; saying with a loud voice, 'Fear God, and give glory to Him, for the hour of His judgment has come; and worship Him who made heaven, and earth, the sea, and springs of water.'"

Then in verse 14 we read: "And I looked, and behold, a white cloud, and on the cloud One like the Son of man, having on his head a golden crown, and in his hand a sharp sickle."

Just before Jesus comes to harvest the earth, an angel's message is sent to the world to warn, "The hour of His judgment is come."

When does this judgment take place? We know that there is a judgment before Jesus comes because the Bible says He will come with rewards. Obviously, if the Lord is prepared to distribute rewards, some form of judgment must precede His return. Doesn't that seem logical to you?

But if that is not enough, Ezekiel 9 also talks about judgment and of angels placing marks on the foreheads of those grieving over sin. Those with marks are spared; those without are destroyed. Verse 6 says, "'Utterly slay old and young men, maidens, and little children, and women; but do not come near anyone on whom is the mark; and begin at My sanctuary.' So they began with the elders who were before the temple."

It was the duty of the angels in Ezekiel to destroy everyone who did not have the mark.

Likewise, the Bible says that in the last days, every person will have a mark, either the seal of God or the mark of the beast. Simply put, those with the seal of God are good and those with the mark of the beast are bad. Ezekiel also hinted that every judgment begins with the house of God. And 1 Peter 4:17 undergirds this truth: "For the time is come for judgment to begin at the house of God; and if it begins with us first, what will be the end of those who do not obey the gospel of God?"

This means God's judgment comes in more than one phase, the first of which, as we have seen, specifically deals with those who claim Christ's name. There are many who "claim" to be cleansed by the blood of Christ. But are we saved based on a "claim" or are we judged by our works? Although it sounds unpopular, the Bible makes it very clear that our works will be evidence of a change of heart. Both the righteous and the unrighteous will be judged according to their works. (See Matthew 12:37; 1 Peter 1:17; Revelation 20:12, 13; 22:12).

Of course, we are not "saved" by our works but by faith through grace (Ephesians 2:5). But Jesus tells us that if we have faith and love Him, we will prove it by leading a different life. We will become holy. We will not be saying, "Lord! Lord!" while living out our own desires (Matthew 7:21–27).

You ask, doesn't God already know who is saved and who is lost? Of course He does, but the judgment isn't for God's benefit! Daniel 7 describes that solemn moment in heaven when "the court is seated, and the books are opened." Here Daniel was permitted to see the relationship between Jesus and the Father, the Ancient of Days, during this special judgment. Jesus is performing His role as our High Priest and pleads our case before the Father and the entire universe. Angels are watching, observing the names of those who have claimed Christ, and are determining if they are genuinely converted. After all, the angels know exactly whether or not our professed loyalty to God is genuine!

Why are the angels so interested in this judgment? The angels know all the names that God has "written" in the Book of Life. These indisputable records reveal to the angels and other unfallen beings that those whose names remain in the Book of Life will be safe to accept into a pure universe. Why? Because they have accepted the gift of Jesus, "the Lamb of God who takes away the sin of the world." This gift of salvation has brought forgiveness and the divine power to transform their hearts.

You may be asking, Why doesn't God start with the wicked in the judgment? Because Jesus said, "I did not come to condemn you. You are condemned already. I came to save you." (See John 3:18–21). Therefore, the cases of the wicked are dealt with in the *last* phase of the judgment, called the *executive judgment,* where sentence is pronounced and executed upon the lost.

That judgment is to be differentiated from the *investigative judgment,* which began in 1844. The investigative judgment is intended for those who have claimed to be faithful loyalists to the Light of Truth.

Revelation considers the seven phases of church history. Of these seven, the church of Laodicea, which means "a judging of the people," is the last. Adventists believe that, during this period, the investigative judgment has been taking place—the one that begins with the house of God. This judgment is also known as the cleansing of the sanctuary that began in 1844.

Obviously, we know that Jesus did not come to earth in 1844 but He did move into the holy of holies phase of His High Priestly ministry. Here begins the heavenly Day of Atonement, so to speak; the final phase of preparing a people who can be trusted with eternal life.

Unfortunately, it is very difficult to prove a theory about what is happening in heaven when you can't see heaven. There are no firsthand witnesses other than the testimony of Scripture. But we do have the Scripture!

THE CLEANSING OF THE BODY—
THE SANCTUARY ON EARTH

Earlier, we established that two sanctuaries remain today and we have seen how Christ began "cleansing" the sanctuary in heaven. Yet is it only the heavenly sanctuary that was to be cleansed or was there something that was to happen on earth? Let's revisit Daniel 8 with this new perspective in mind. Here Daniel describes a remarkable antagonist who does great mischief in confusing the truths about the plan of salvation and the character of God. This power would not be merely the act of one man, but of a system developed over many years.

This remarkable power would cast "truth to the ground" while it passed itself off as a religious power that would capture the loyalty of earth's millions. The true church would go through a difficult period until the time when "the sanctuary" should be "cleansed." Many today have mistakenly taken these words in Daniel 8 to mean that the antichrist will rebuild the literal temple in Jerusalem, without understanding that it is God's people, not brick and mortar, who now constitute the temple of God. Believers are the living stones resting upon the Great Cornerstone.

So when the Bible says that the "wicked one will sit in the temple of God showing himself that he is god" (2 Thessalonians 2:4), it is talking about a formidable religio-political power that exerts control over much of Christianity, while asserting that it is deserving of worship. This power did not literally enter a physical temple, but established itself at the center of the Christian church.

How has the earthly "temple" been defiled? It was defiled from false doctrines—pure gospel truth was cast to the ground, obscured, distorted, and diluted. But God had a plan to restore the faith that was once delivered to the saints. He would cleanse the church on earth from the false doctrines that had compromised its purity over the centuries.

Now, let's examine the importance of the time after 1844. Those who had not lost their confidence in God (because of the Great Disappointment) delved into the Scriptures even more deeply. Even though they did not understand why God did not come, they laid aside their disappointments and denominational barriers to allow the Holy Spirit to guide them to the truth. Soon, this small group of believers — again, from several denominations—rediscovered, among other long-forsaken Bible truths, the seventh-day Sabbath, baptism by immersion, the truth about the state of the dead, and that their bodies were the temple of the Holy Spirit.

From every corner of the earth, God brought His people together into a great melting pot, and said, "I am going to cleanse my church."

I cannot prove precisely what happened in heaven, but I can prove that God started to cleanse His earthly sanctuary, beginning as early as 1844.

A FALSE PEACE, AND A TRUE HEART

However, during this period of time, a doctrine emerged that has caused much misunderstanding. That doctrine is: "once saved, always saved." Often, when I have explained that the judgment of the church is included in the cleansing of the sanctuary, people have objected, "Wait! The church has already been saved!"

Such thinking is clearly unbiblical. The Bible is clear: When people are converted, their names are written in the Book of Life (Philippians 4:3; Revelation 13:8); but those names can also be removed—blotted out—if necessary (Revelation 3:5; 22:19).

Wouldn't you like to believe that once your name is written in the Book of Life, it can never be removed? But that doesn't make sense. In America, just because a person gains citizenship, this doesn't mean that he is free to disobey the laws of the land. He is held accountable, even more so as a citizen!

In Exodus 32:33, God said to Moses: "Whoever has sinned against Me, I will blot him out of My book." God is referring to His chosen people, people who later sinned against Him. Jesus Himself said: "He who overcomes shall be clothed in white garments, and I will not blot out his name from the Book of Life; but I will confess his name before My Father and before His angels" (Revelation 3:5). Again, you can see how involved the angels are in how the plan of salvation plays out in our rebellious world!

Salvation is not just a divine cover-up, or a legal transaction conducted by a forgiving God. It is a dynamic process that transforms sinners to loyal followers of the Lord Jesus. The Bible is loaded with promises, such as "He who overcomes shall inherit all things, and I shall be his God and he shall be My son" (Revelation 21:7); and "To him who overcomes I will grant to sit with Me on My throne, as I also overcame and sat down with My Father on His throne" (Revelation 3:21).

Planet Earth is the theater of the universe—the object of intense focus of all the unfallen worlds and angels, who are watching to see if God can fulfill His promise that He will have a people to whom He can again entrust eternal life. To facilitate this, God obviously has an immaculate record-keeping system that is beyond our comprehension. (Still, I can't help but wonder if it's some kind of visual panorama, like those He's given the prophets—with instant video call-up for any year since creation, for any person at any moment in his or her life.)

I can't know that yet, but I do know that the Bible says that people will be judged by their deeds written in the books. (These books of deeds are obviously different from the Book of Life.) For example, Jesus said in Matthew 12: "Don't you know that you will give an account in the judgment for every idle word that you speak?" That makes me tremble! He says,

"For by your words you will be justified and by your words you will be condemned." Words show what is in our hearts, and it is according to what is in our hearts that we will be judged.

When I catch myself speaking badly of another person, I ask myself, "What's wrong with my heart?" When you ask God to forgive your sins and place your name in His Book of Life, you are telling Him that you are weak and unable to make it on your own. This pledge of submission represents a transformation of the heart. With that one simple pledge, you give Jesus permission to work on your heart and add your name to the Book of Life. He is the Author and Finisher of your faith, and you can believe that God always finishes whatever He starts, if we continue to give Him permission.

Righteousness by faith is knowing that you are forgiven, and understanding that Christ as your High Priest lives to empower you by His grace. It is knowing that you are a temple, and that Jesus through the Holy Spirit is dwelling within you. That is why the sanctuary doctrine is so powerful and life-transforming. It's a concept you don't have to guess about. God will cleanse the sanctuary within you just as He cleansed the earthly temple. To the extent that He is cleansing His people and making them overcomers, He is cleansing His heavenly sanctuary. One is a mirror of the other! Yet Christ will not force His presence upon those who refuse His offer. He will ultimately be forced to walk away and say, "Your house is left unto you desolate."

MICHAEL STANDS

Life on earth will continue for a short time after the investigative judgment has finished, but it will not be a comfortable environment. The plagues of Revelation and the great time of trouble begin after the judgment that began in 1844 ends. Daniel wrote: "At that time Michael shall stand up, the great prince who stands watch over the sons of your people" (Daniel 12:1, 2). Michael (which is another name for Christ), will no longer be listening to evidence once the investigative judgment is over. At that time, all cases will be closed. Daniel continued:

> "There shall be a time of trouble, such as never was since there was a nation even to that time. And at that time your people shall be delivered, everyone who is found written in the book. And many of those who sleep in the dust of the earth shall awake, some to everlasting life, some to shame and everlasting contempt."

In Noah's time, life continued for seven days after he entered the ark with his family and before the rain came. But the storm did come, too late now for those outside the boat. The doors of the ark had been long sealed.

Regarding the end-time just before us, John wrote: "The temple was filled with smoke from the glory of God, and from his power, and no one was able to enter the temple till the seven plagues of the seven angels were completed" (Revelation 15:8). I praise God that you and I are able to go by faith into that temple today.

The Bible says that you and I, by faith in our Lord's keeping power, may go boldly before the throne of God (Hebrews 4:14–16). Yet someday soon the door of mercy will be closed against those who continue to refuse our Lord's repeated invitations. When that door is closed, where will we be able to go for cleansing? Perhaps this is why Paul says in Hebrews: "How shall we escape if we neglect so great a salvation?" (Hebrews 2:3). Now is the time to go before the throne of God and ask for cleansing, mercy and grace, before the door of mercy is closed forever (see Hebrews 4:16).

Jesus said in Revelation 22:11: "He who is unjust, let him be unjust still; he who is filthy, let him be filthy still." The good news is that a time is coming when the righteous will not have to worry about becoming dirty again, as Jesus continued: "He who is righteous, let him be righteous still; he who is holy, let him be holy still." When you invite Christ into your heart and mind, you become a living sanctuary. He will dwell in your soul temple and cast out all of the moneychangers and the beasts and everything else that defiles you. In Romans 12:1, Paul made this appeal: "I beseech you therefore, brethren, by the mercies of God, that you present your bodies a living sacrifice, holy, acceptable to God, which is your reasonable service." When the time comes for Jesus to arrive and take you home to be His forever friend, you will hear Him whisper in your ear, "Well done, my good and faithful servant."

How can we doubt that the message of the sanctuary, recognized almost exclusively by the Seventh-day Adventist church, is full of hope and possibilities for all of Christ's faithful here on earth?

Chapter Six

ADVENTISTS AND THE AFTERLIFE

The subject of death is always shrouded with sadness, relief, and superstition. Sadness because someone we love is no longer by our side, relief because they have found rest from the troubles of the world, and superstition because so many opinions exist as to where the dead now are. Yet Christians need not be smothered by sadness, despair or fear because God offers a gift that provides more than just a glimmer of hope. The Scriptures offer real peace to a heart that is restless and unsure about the end of life.

Seventh-day Adventists embrace an often unpopular view of death that is slightly different than the view held by other mainstream churches. In this chapter, we will explore what the Bible has to say about death and show clearly why Adventism's view about the state of the dead is not only biblical, it also lacks the superstitious flavor of popular Christian belief. We call it "the blessed hope" (Titus 2:13).

SUPERSTITION

Around the city of San Jose, California, you can spot all kinds of signs pointing tourists toward the Winchester Mystery House. The story of Sarah Pardee Winchester, widow of William W. Winchester, the wealthy heir to the Winchester Repeating Rifle Manufacturing Company that produced thousands of guns during the Civil War, is one of the strangest true stories in America.

In 1866, the Winchester family announced the birth of their daughter Annie, their first child. But their profound joy soon turned to tragedy when Annie became sick and died six months after her birth. Shortly after, Mr. Winchester died of tuberculosis, leaving a shattered Sarah alone and in despair. Distraught, and desperate for answers, Sarah visited a Boston psychic who said a curse had been placed on the Winchester family because of all the people who had been killed by the family rifle business.

The medium also told Sarah that in order to appease these angry spirits and achieve everlasting life, she must move west and begin building a house, and never stop building. So Sarah took her $20 million cash inheritance and $1000 a day income and moved west to California in 1884. Believing the spirits could do no harm to her if she did as the psychic said, Sarah began building. She bought an unfinished eight-room farmhouse near San Jose, and quickly employed a staff that included carpenters that worked seven days a week, 24 hours a day. When she ran out of space, she tore down rooms and had new ones built. It has been estimated that she had more than 600 rooms built during the span of her lifetime. During those 38 years, the house grew into a sprawling structure covering 5 acres with 160 rooms, 13 bathrooms, 6 kitchens, 40 staircases, 47 fireplaces, 2,000 doors and 10,000 windows. Her home has since become known as the Winchester Mystery House.

Of course, Sarah isn't the only person who has been tormented by confusion about the state of the dead. If she had known what the Bible says, she would have found lasting peace and more fully understood God's plan of salvation for her. It would also have been easier for her to see through the fraud perpetrated against her—the same fraud believed, not only by most non-Christians, but by most Christians the world over.

Revelation 16 describes three unclean spirits that come out of the mouth of "the beast," "the dragon," and "the false prophet." We're warned that these spirits of devils will be working overtime to deceive the kings of the earth by performing miracles and by bringing the whole world to the battle of the great day of God—the battle of Armageddon.

I find it disconcerting that even world leaders today are consulting astrologers and mediums to get advice on how to proceed with their nation's business. Are these last-day deceptions of Revelation 16 being fulfilled right now? Christians must be especially vigilant, because we are the special targets of these unclean spirits.

A DEATH FOR EVERY PERSONALITY

In the Bible, more than a thousand references to death can be found. One of the most philosophical is in Ecclesiastes 3:1, 2, which says, "To everything there is a season, A time for every purpose under heaven: A time to be born, and a time to die." Paul affirmed this in Hebrews, saying, "It is appointed for men to die once, but after this the judgment" (9:27). Everyone dies if they live long enough. (How's that for a profound thought!)

Job asks a deeply penetrating question that goes something like this: "If a man dies, shall he live again?" (Job 14:14). Many different people have attempted to answer that question. For instance, some humanistic philosophers assert that when you die, it's just a part of the "circle of life," and we all become compost that in turn feeds the trees of the forest and the grass eaten by animals. In a sense, one lives on through an orange or an apple in a complex earth-as-god religion. I don't know about you, but I don't find that very satisfying.

I once very sincerely believed in reincarnation. My friends and I often spent hours discussing our "former lives." They were never average Joe's, of course, but famous people like Cleopatra or Napoleon. But it always bugged me that I could never remember any of my past lives—what good was that to me?

The Bible's version of life after death is a distant relative of Hindu or Buddhist reincarnation. It refers to this life as a kind of boot camp for the world to come, and says that those who die will live again. Other than that, though, the Bible's form of rebirth is far removed from multiple reincarnations that go and on. Indeed, the Bible clearly states that this life is the only opportunity we have to choose our eternal destiny. This is why it is so important that we understand that the choices we make in our own brief, and sometimes difficult, life are the deciding factors that determine where we will spend eternity.

DEATH UNCOVERED

The very first lie in the Bible was spoken by the serpent in Genesis 3:4. This lie was about death, and it has permeated religious thought in the centuries since. The serpent said, "You will not surely die." Of course, in the New Testament, Paul counters, "[God] alone has immortality" (1 Timothy 6:16).

With those two verses in mind, let's consider two extreme thoughts about death that are being circulated today, and what the Bible has to say about them. One extreme states that when you die your body turns to dirt and remains so forever. The other extreme states that you are immortal (that is, your "soul"), and thus cannot die. This last line of thought dates back to the Garden of Eden and probably rates as the biggest lie ever told in history.

So what does the Bible have to say about what happens when a person dies? Ecclesiastes 12:7 is clear: "Then the dust will return to the earth as it was, and the spirit [breath] will return to God who gave it." This verse has often been used to assert that, while a person's body might decompose at death, his spirit, which is interpreted to mean a conscious soul, returns to God. However, Ecclesiastes also says that the spirit of the animals, such as cats, dogs, birds and bees—which are clearly amoral creatures—also returns to God who gave it (see Ecclesiastes 3:19).

So what is a "spirit"? In Ecclesiastes, it obviously means "the breath of life." This does not support the idea of instant heaven or hell after death—far from it. Is this consistent with the rest of the Bible? Genesis 2:7 records that God formed man from the dust of the earth and breathed into his nostrils the breath of life—and man *became* a living soul. Much of the confusion afflicting the world and Christians arises from the notion that man has a soul that functions distinctly from his body, but the Bible flatly rejects this, calling man himself a soul. So when death occurs, the exact opposite of what happened at creation occurs—the body returns to dust and the breath of life goes back to God.

The Bible also explains that the dead are "sleeping" and will continue to be in that state until the resurrection takes place. Daniel 12:2 says: "And many of those who sleep in the dust of the earth shall awake, some to everlasting life, some to shame and everlasting contempt." Job 14:12 confirms this: "So man lies down, and does not rise. Till the heavens be no more, they will not awake nor be roused from their sleep."

The New Testament is just as consistent as the old. In the Gospel of John, the phrase "last days" is used seven times, often in relation to the resurrection. For example, Jesus said in John 6:39: "This is the will of Him who sent Me, that everyone who sees the Son and believes in Him may have everlasting life; and I will raise him up at the last day." What "last day" is being referred to here—the last day of a person's life, or the end of the world? Jesus clearly means the end of the world.

How does the Bible refer to death? From Moses to Daniel, to Jesus to Paul, the Bible calls death a sleep. Remember when Jesus said that Lazarus, who had been dead for several days, was "sleeping" (see John 11:11–14)? No biblical text ever mentions anything about the dead being in purgatory or limbo, nor does it teach that people are in torment or glory. All it ever says is that the dead are in a painless, dreamless, and uneventful sleep.

THE RESURRECTION

One of the most convincing Scriptures about the timing of the resurrection is found in 1 Corinthians 15:20–23. The Corinthians had serious problems regarding the issues of speaking in tongues and proper worship. Paul went to great lengths to clarify those, and other key issues for them, including the resurrection. He taught, "But now Christ is risen from the dead, and has become the firstfruits of those who have fallen asleep. For since by man came death, by Man also came the resurrection of the dead. For as in Adam all die, even so in Christ all shall be made alive."

In 1 Thessalonians 4:13–18, Paul was emphatic: "But I would not want you to be ignorant, brethren, concerning those have fallen asleep." Paul is as clear as the noon-day sun: dead people are still waiting for their resurrection.

He continued: "For if we believe that Jesus died and rose again, even so God will bring with Him those who sleep in Jesus."

People have argued, "Now wait, Doug! It says He's going to bring them with Him. They're already with Him, so they are coming with Him." But this text doesn't say that—we merely need to read on: "For this we say to you by the word of the Lord, that we who are alive and remain until the coming of the Lord will by no means precede those who are asleep." In other words, those who are alive when Jesus returns will not go to heaven before those who are asleep in Christ— meaning that those who have died still need to wake up at the call of the Life Giver.

Paul now provides the sequence of events for the resurrection day: "For the Lord Himself will descend from heaven with a shout, with the voice of an archangel, and with the trumpet of God. And the dead in Christ will rise first."

When shall the dead in Christ rise? He will raise them at His coming. As Paul said, "Then we who are alive and remain shall be caught up together with them in the clouds, to meet the Lord in the air. And thus we shall always be with the Lord. Therefore comfort one another with these words."

BE NOT DECEIVED

After reading all this, you might be wondering why it is so important to understand the state of the dead and the biblical sequence of events regarding the end-times and the raising of the dead back to life. It's important for us to understand all this, for the same reason that it was important for Sarah Pardee Winchester to understand—we must have peace regarding those who are dead and not be worried about being cursed by ghosts from the past.

But even more important—when demons (Revelation 16:13) go out to deceive the kings of the earth in the last days, they will impersonate loved ones in order to convey "guidance" that is contrary to the Scriptures. If you and I know that the dead are asleep in a dreamless, unconscious state, we will be on our guard against what would otherwise be an overwhelming deception.

Let's look again at the inconsistency of believing that our dead loved ones are either in heaven or hell. Some say that Jesus is coming back only to resurrect the body, but that doesn't make sense: We are told that we will receive new bodies at the resurrection. Why wait to give them new bodies if they are already in heaven or hell?

Let's push this issue a little further. What would be the purpose of a Judgment Day if people were already consigned to heaven or hell? Revelation 22:12 quotes Jesus' clear statement: "Behold, I am coming quickly, and My reward is with Me, to give to every one according to his work."

When does the Bible say that Jesus will give rewards? "When He comes." But if a good person dies and goes straight to Paradise or if a bad person goes straight to hell, what more could Jesus give to them when He returns to earth? Would He judge them all over again? But that doesn't make any sense.

Let's look again at the death of Lazarus. Jesus plainly referred to death as a sleep shortly before He resurrected Lazarus. John 11:11 records: "'Our friend Lazarus sleeps; but I go that I may wake him up.' Then his disciples said, 'Lord, if he sleeps, he shall do well.'" The disciples were confused by Jesus' terminology, until He plainly stated, "Lazarus is dead!" In other words, Lazarus had no idea what was going on; he was sleeping the sleep of death.

In addition to Lazarus, the Bible mentions many other people who died and were eventually resurrected, including Moses, the boy brought to life by Elijah, Jarius' daughter, and the "many bodies of the saints who had fallen asleep," (that is, "died" in Old Testament times). Soon after Jesus was resurrected, these saints appeared in Jerusalem (see Matthew 27:52, 53). Although these individuals were definitely reported as having been dead, I find it interesting that not one of them recounts their experience while in "heaven"—or, I suppose, "hell" for that matter. Can you imagine being snatched down from heaven to be resurrected on earth? "Thank you very much, but do you expect me to leave heaven and come back to this crazy world?"

Everyone today wonders what heaven is like. Do you think it was any different in biblical times? All the friends and family members of those saints who had been dead would have been asking them what it was like, yet the Bible remains silent on their experiences after death! Did Lazarus not have anything to share? Ecclesiastes 9:5 says they wouldn't: "The living know that they will die: but the dead know nothing." Not only do the dead know nothing; they can't haunt you!

ABSENT FROM THE BODY?

For the most part, the Bible is very clear about the subject of death—no confusing statements, no fuzzy pictures. But several biblical texts have become favorite rifle shots aimed at Adventist teaching and the church itself. Let's look at the most often used texts that some find confusing.

One of these is 2 Corinthians 5:8, 9: "We are confident, yes, well pleased rather to be absent from the body and to be present with the Lord. Therefore we make it our aim, whether present or absent, to be well pleasing to Him." This is a verse that I questioned often in my spiritual journey.

Just before Paul died, he wrote: "The time of my departure is at hand. I have fought the good fight." Paul looked forward to the crown of righteousness that the Lord would be giving him, but did he really say he would receive it instantly after death? Of course not! He said that the crown would be given to him "on that Day, and not to me only but also to all who have loved His appearing" (2 Timothy 4:7, 8). This is the same "Day" that Paul referred to in 1 Thessalonians 4:14–18. Paul is clear and consistent: we will all be caught up *together*, meaning that we won't be alone when we come out of the grave.

If you are a Christian who is about to die, or if you were the apostle Paul soon to be beheaded by Nero, what would be your next conscious thought? The first thing you will be aware of after death will be hearing the Voice of the Lifegiver calling you to "Awake!" You will hear and see the angels uniting loved ones—it will all occur virtually instantaneously. When does this happen? "In a moment, in the twinkling of an eye at the last trumpet." At the last trumpet Paul and the rest of the dead in Christ will rise from the grave and know that they are in the presence of God and surrounded by their loved ones.

Now back to our problem text in 2 Corinthians 5. I admit this is a difficult passage at first glance. At least, it is ambiguous.

But if we choose to believe that Paul meant instant transport to heaven after death, then we must choose to believe that all his other statements are false. We should make this text fit all of His other clear statements—just to be fair to Paul. But before we look at this passage more carefully, we must ask this question: is it really safe to build a doctrine on one passage of Scripture? Isn't it better to see how that passage can be understood in the light of the enormous weight of the rest of the Bible? I think so.

What Paul is saying in 2 Corinthians 5 is that he earnestly desired to be with the Lord—he is growing tired after years of non-stop ministry. He would be pleased to avoid death altogether; that is, he hopes to avoid the state of being "naked," or "unclothed," and go to heaven without seeing death (verses 2–4). Obviously Paul does not think of death as being a disembodied spirit; rather he sees death as an intermediate state of being "naked" or "unclothed." As he explains in his other statements regarding the resurrection when Jesus returns to earth, only then will he be "clothed" and his "mortality be swallowed up." (See 1 Corinthians 15, and 1 Thessalonians 4.)

THOSE WHO HAVE GONE BEFORE

We have a few examples of Bible characters who have gone before us. Enoch walked with God (Genesis 5:24) and God took him directly (translated) to heaven. Elijah was also translated and left the earth in a chariot of fire (2 Kings 2). Moses was not translated as were Enoch and Elijah, but he received a special resurrection in which Michael came to escort him to heaven (Jude 9). Both Moses and Elijah returned to earth and met with Jesus on the Mount of Transfiguration—what a meeting that was (Matthew 17)!

Earlier, we mentioned the Old Testament saints who were raised to life when Jesus was—what a story they had to tell (Matthew 27)! God provided for these exceptions because they were fulfilling an important part of the plan of salvation.

During harvest time in the Old Testament days, the High Priest took a portion of the first harvest of grain and waved it before the Lord as an offering—a type of what Jesus would do after His resurrection. Christ "waved" these resurrected saints before the universe as the first yield of the gospel harvest; He presented them before God after His ascension into the heavens. In Revelation 5:8, we read about the 24 elders who are probably some of those who were resurrected on that glorious Sunday morning and are now surrounding the throne of God.

JESUS AND THE THIEF IN PARADISE

Another controversial passage used to support the notion of an instant passage into heaven or hell is the story of the thief who was crucified beside Jesus. Luke 23:42, 43 gives the beautiful account of this eleventh-hour conversion. After defending Jesus' innocence, the thief cries out to Him, "Lord, remember me when You come into Your kingdom." The conversion is absolutely genuine. The thief confesses his sinful condition and, in a moment, understands in outline the entire plan of salvation. In spite of all Christ's sufferings that day, the humiliation and the beatings, He turns instantly to this repentant sinner and says, "Assuredly, I say to you today you will be with Me in Paradise." That seems pretty clear, doesn't it? "Today you and I will be together in Paradise."

But there's one problem! When this passage was written in Greek, the Bible writers used no form of punctuation. When the verse was translated into English, the punctuation as we know it was inserted at the discretion of the translators. The translators added the commas in your English Bible! That one little comma can make a world of difference in the meaning of Luke 23:43.

A woman who went on a Paris holiday telegraphed her husband on her birthday and asked him if she could buy herself a fur coat for $2000. He responded with a telegram that read, "No price too high." At the end of her vacation, she disembarked from the ship and strolled toward her husband. He saw that she was wearing a beautiful, white mink stole, and said, "I told you not to buy that coat! It was too expensive!" As it turned out, the telegraph operator omitted a comma—the message should have read: "No, price too high." A single comma changed the meaning completely!

This is what happened in Luke's passage. The translator would have retained Christ's meaning if he had withheld the comma: "Assuredly, I say to you today you will be with Me in Paradise." Inserting that comma before "today" causes the passage to contradict everything the Bible teaches on the subject. But leave it out and it instantly conforms to all other passages.

But the Bible provides additional circumstantial evidence to show why moving or omitting that comma makes sense. John records that when Mary Magdalene clung to Jesus' feet when she saw Him for the first time that Sunday morning, Jesus instructed her, "Do not cling to Me, for I have not yet ascended to My Father" (20:17). Two days had passed since Jesus' death, and He still had not seen His Father in Paradise. How could Jesus and the thief on the cross have been in Paradise on Friday?

Christ did not look like a king when the thief on the cross addressed Him. In fact, all who were standing around Him were saying, "He is defeated."

Here is what Christ was really saying to the thief: "I know I don't look like much right now, but today I am making you a promise. You are going to be with me in Paradise." Some translations actually render the punctuation correctly.

ARE OUR LOVED ONES WATCHING US?

Psalm 146 is another passage that illustrates the true state of man in death: "Do not put your trust in princes, nor in a son of man, in whom there is no help. His spirit departs, he returns to his earth; In that very day his plans perish" (verses 3, 4). This teaches us that when a person dies, he stops thinking. It surprises me that we are so easily lured into spiritualism. You can hardly turn on the television without seeing at least one or two commercials advertising psychics or shows fully devoted to communication with the dead. Obviously there is a market large enough to sustain this sensationalism or the industry would not be thriving.

But is it possible to receive visits from loved ones who have passed away? I have often heard people say, "Grandma has died, but I feel that she is with me."

Our brains are extraordinary computers; we have a lot of information stored back there on our hard drive. Memories of our loved ones are stored deep in our minds. They are close to us emotionally, near our hearts, but they are not present physically.

After my brother died I would open my eyes and reach out toward his flaming red hair and brown eyes. We grew up together. Never was there a time when Falcon was not around. After he died, he still seemed alive and tangible to me, even though he was gone.

I will never forget the day that I picked up the phone to call him even though he would not be there to answer. What caused that? Was Falcon trying to communicate with me? No. I was the one who wanted desperately to be near him. It was perhaps a part of the grieving process that can get out of hand when people don't know what the Bible really says.

Likewise, many people claim to have had so-called near-death experiences, in which they are transported to the gates of heaven only to be suddenly pulled back. But can we base our conclusions on the subjective accounts of people who were experiencing a certain amount of brain trauma from lack of oxygen or some other neurological anomaly? Too many people want to base their theology on someone's deathbed experience—but if you believe the Bible, you will believe that the dead are resting and know nothing at all. We need to show appreciation to our families now—not wait to honor them with flowers at their funerals, because they won't be able to appreciate it then. Let them know that you love them today, while you have the chance to touch their lives.

WHY HOPE DOESN'T DIE

Death was not a part of God's plan for us. Most people will eventually die, but the promises of God should alleviate our fears and our worries. You know, we are living in the last generation, and some of us will not die. Doesn't that excite you? I certainly am hoping to be alive when Christ returns, just as 1 Corinthians 15:51 says, "Behold, I tell you a mystery: We shall not all sleep, but we shall all be changed."

That's right! Changed! No believer will be going to heaven with his or her old body. The Bible says that in the twinkling of an eye, at the last trumpet, the dead will be raised incorruptible, with glorified bodies that will not age. Getting old is scary. I am starting to feel my mortality—the aches and pains and creaking bones hit me a little more after a game of racquetball. One of my friends said to me: "It gets to the point where, when you bend over to pick something up and you say to yourself, what else can I pick up while I am down here."

Death is the enemy, but the Bible says that Christians do not die—they sleep. The Bible even tells us that King David is still asleep. Acts 2:29 says: "Men and brethren, let me speak freely to you of the patriarch David, that he is both dead and buried, and his tomb is with us to this day."

Will it seem to David that he has been sleeping for 3,000 years when he is resurrected? No, it will seem like an instant has transpired between his last earthly thoughts and the moment when the trumpet blows. No longer an old, tired man, he will rise from the grave in a glorified body, if his name remains in the Book of Life.

We all have the opportunity to sing with the resurrected saints: "O Death, where is your sting? O Hades, where is your victory?" (1 Corinthians 15:55). Death and the grave will be cast into the lake of fire (Revelation 20:14). Revelation 21:4 promises: "And God will wipe away every tear from their eyes." No longer will death rule! No longer will everything that is alive be expected to die.

In a sinful world, we are never far from death. Every news broadcast reminds us that death hurts and is scary—if not, why do so many people fear it? But one day that will all change. We will live in a world where nothing dies. I like the way the Bible succinctly says, "No more death" (Revelation 21:4).

Isn't that good news! I am tired of death. I am tired of attending funerals for family members and friends whom I love. I am looking forward to the day when the trumpet shall sound and the dead in Christ shall rise and we will be caught up together on the way to heaven.

I hope you will draw comfort from these words, because it is not necessary to fear death. The Adventist message not only explains the truth about death, it offers a hope that no other message can offer. With Paul and Titus, we can call it "the blessed hope" (Titus 2:13). Someday soon, there will be no more good-byes, no more funerals, no more death. Just eternal sunshine and eternal fellowship with our loved ones and with God! Truly, we have "a blessed hope!"